New York C Guide 202

Insider Tips, Must-See Sights, Experiences and Adventures in the Empire City

Evelyn Blair

Map Of New York City

Scan the QR code to see the map of New York City

Table of Contents

INTRODUCTION

Planning a trip to New York City can be a daunting task. With its vast size and endless options, it's easy to feel overwhelmed by the choices. Many travellers end up missing out on important details that could make their trip smoother and more enjoyable.

This guidebook is here to solve that problem. It offers clear and practical advice to make your visit to New York City easier and more enjoyable. You'll find valuable insights on everything from must-see landmarks to lesser-known treasures, tailored for solo travellers, couples, families, and more.

This guide is based on well-researched and accurate information. The advice provided is designed to help you navigate the city confidently, ensuring you have a great experience.

By following the tips in this book, you'll save time and avoid common pitfalls. You'll know where to go, what to do, and how to plan your days so that you can enjoy your trip to the fullest.

Countless travellers have found that having a clear plan makes a huge difference. This guide will provide you with the insights needed to make your trip smooth and enjoyable.

This book will help you make the most of your visit to New York City, ensuring you have a memorable and stress-free experience.

The sooner you start preparing, the better your trip will be. Don't wait until the last minute to get the information you need.
Continue reading to find everything you need to plan a successful and enjoyable trip to New York City.

The Origins and Growth of New York City

New York, one of the world's most iconic and influential cities, has a fascinating history that spans several centuries. Its journey from a small settlement to a bustling metropolis is a story of exploration, trade, immigration, and transformation.

The story begins in the early 1600s, when European explorers first arrived in the area now known as New York. In 1609, an English explorer named Henry Hudson, working for the Dutch East India Company, navigated his ship, the Half Moon, into what is now New York Harbor. His exploration of the river, which now bears his name, opened the door for European interest in the region.

Shortly after Hudson's voyage, the Dutch established a trading post at the southern tip of Manhattan Island in 1624. They named this settlement New Amsterdam. It served primarily as a hub for the fur trade, where the Dutch traded goods like beads and metal tools with the Native American tribes in exchange for animal pelts. Over time, New Amsterdam grew into a small but thriving community, attracting settlers from various parts of Europe.

New Amsterdam's location at the mouth of the Hudson River made it a strategically important settlement for the Dutch. The town's position allowed it to control access to the inland regions, which were rich in resources. However, its strategic importance also made it a target for rival powers. In 1664, the English seized control of New Amsterdam without much resistance. They renamed the city New York in honour of the Duke of York, who later became King James II of England.

Under English rule, New York expanded rapidly. The city became a key port for the British colonies in America. Ships from around the world docked in New York, bringing goods, people, and ideas. The city's population grew as immigrants arrived from Europe, seeking new opportunities in the New World. New York's diversity began to take shape, with people of different backgrounds, languages, and religions settling in the city.

During the 18th century, New York played a significant role in the events leading up to the American Revolution. The city was a centre of political and military activity, and it became a battleground during the war for independence. After the revolution, New York briefly served as the capital of the newly formed United States. It was during this time that George Washington took the oath of office as the first President of the United States on the balcony of Federal Hall, located on Wall Street.

The 19th century brought tremendous growth and change to New York City. The opening of the Erie Canal in 1825 connected New York to the Great Lakes, making the city a vital link between the Atlantic Ocean and the interior of North America. The canal's success spurred economic growth, attracting more immigrants and fuelling the city's expansion. New York became the financial and commercial centre of the United States, a status it still holds today.

As the city grew, it also faced challenges. Overcrowding, poverty, and disease became significant issues as more people flocked to New York in search of better lives. Despite these difficulties, the city continued to thrive. The late 19th and early 20th centuries saw the construction of iconic landmarks such as the Statue of Liberty, a gift from France that became a symbol of freedom and democracy, and the Brooklyn Bridge, a marvel of engineering that connected Manhattan and Brooklyn.

New York City continued to evolve in the 20th century. The city's skyline transformed with the construction of skyscrapers like the Empire State Building and the Chrysler Building. These towering structures became symbols of New York's ambition and innovation. The city also became a cultural capital, attracting artists, writers, musicians, and performers from around the world.

Throughout the century, New York faced various challenges, including economic downturns, crime, and social unrest. However, the city always found ways to reinvent itself. It became a melting pot of cultures, where people from all over the world lived and worked side by side. This diversity gave rise to vibrant neighbourhoods, each with its own unique character.

Today, New York City is a global centre for finance, culture, and entertainment. Its influence extends far beyond its five boroughs, shaping trends and ideas around the world. The city's history is a testament to its resilience and its ability to adapt to changing times. From its early days as a Dutch trading post to its current status as a global metropolis, New York City has always been a place of opportunity, where anything seems possible.

How to Use This Guide

This guide is designed to make your visit to New York City as smooth and enjoyable as possible. The information is organised to help you find what you need easily, whether you're planning your trip, navigating the city, or looking for things to do.

You'll find detailed explanations about various aspects of New York City, including where to go, what to see, and how to get around. The guide provides practical advice on choosing accommodations, finding the best attractions, and making the most of your time in the city. It also includes essential tips for staying safe, understanding local customs, and preparing for your visit.

Throughout the guide, you'll see references to specific locations, attractions, and landmarks. To help you find these places easily, maps are included in the form of QR codes. These QR codes can be scanned with your smartphone, giving you access to detailed maps directly on your device. You can use your phone's camera app or a QR code reader app to scan these codes. Once scanned, the map will appear on your screen, showing you the exact location and helping you navigate to it.

In addition to the maps, this guide also includes pictures to give you a visual idea of what to expect. These images are carefully selected to complement the information provided, helping you to recognise landmarks and get a feel for different areas of the city.

As you read through the guide, use the maps and pictures to enhance your understanding of the city and plan your itinerary. This guide offers the tools and information you need to make informed decisions.

By following the advice given and using the maps and pictures provided, you can ensure that your trip to New York City is well- organised and filled with memorable experiences.

CHAPTER 1

Planning Your Trip

Before embarking on your journey to New York City, a bit of preparation goes a long way. Planning ahead will not only help you make the most of your time in the city but also ensure a smoother and more enjoyable experience. Here, you'll find essential information to help you get ready for your trip, from understanding the city's climate and cultural norms to knowing what to pack and what documents you'll need. With the right preparation, you can step into New York City feeling confident and ready to explore.

The City's Climate and Choosing the Best Time to Visit

New York City experiences a wide range of weather conditions throughout the year, with each season offering its own unique atmosphere and opportunities for visitors. Understanding the city's climate can help you plan your trip more effectively and ensure that you experience the city in the way that best suits your preferences.

New York City has a humid subtropical climate, which means that it experiences four distinct seasons: spring, summer, fall, and winter. The city's location on the northeastern coast of the United States influences its weather patterns, with temperatures varying significantly between seasons.

Spring in New York City is a time of renewal and growth. It typically begins in late March and lasts through May. During this period, temperatures gradually rise from the cooler conditions of winter, making the days more comfortable for exploring the city. Early spring can be quite chilly, with temperatures often ranging from 40°F to 60°F (4°C to 15°C). As the season progresses, the weather becomes milder, with average daytime temperatures reaching between 60°F and 75°F (15°C to 24°C). Spring is also known for its blooming flowers and budding trees, particularly in the city's many parks, such as Central Park. This season is ideal for outdoor activities and sightseeing, as the weather is generally pleasant and the city is less crowded than during the peak summer months.

Summer in New York City, which lasts from June through August, is characterised by warm to hot temperatures and higher humidity levels. Average daytime temperatures range from 75°F to 85°F (24°C to 29°C), although it's not uncommon for temperatures to exceed 90°F (32°C) during heatwaves. The city can feel particularly warm due to the "urban heat island" effect, where buildings and pavement absorb and retain heat, making the environment feel hotter than surrounding rural areas. Summer is a popular time to visit New York City because of the longer daylight hours and the wide variety of outdoor events, festivals, and concerts that take place. However, it's also the busiest tourist season, so popular attractions may be more crowded. If visiting during the summer, it's advisable to stay hydrated and take breaks in air-conditioned spaces to stay comfortable.

Fall, which occurs from September through November, is one of the most picturesque times to visit New York City. The season is marked by cooler temperatures, lower humidity, and the stunning transformation of the city's foliage. Early fall still retains some of summer's warmth, with temperatures ranging from 65°F to 75°F (18°C to 24°C). As the season progresses, temperatures drop, and by November, they typically range from 45°F to 60°F (7°C to 15°C). The changing leaves in the city's parks and along tree-lined streets create a vibrant display of reds, oranges, and yellows, making it a favourite time for both locals and visitors. Fall is also a great time to enjoy outdoor activities like walking tours, bike rides, and exploring the city's markets. The weather is generally comfortable, and the city tends to be less crowded than in summer, making it an excellent time for sightseeing.

Winter in New York City lasts from December through February and brings colder temperatures, shorter daylight hours, and the possibility of snow. Average daytime temperatures during winter range from 30°F to 45°F (-1°C to 7°C), though it can feel colder with the wind chill. Snowfall is common, particularly in January and February, with the city experiencing several snowstorms each year. Winter in New York City has its own charm, with festive holiday decorations, ice skating rinks, and seasonal markets creating a magical atmosphere. Popular attractions like Rockefeller Centre, with its famous Christmas tree, and the ice skating rink in Central Park draw visitors from all over the world. While winter can be cold and sometimes snowy, it's a great time to experience the city's holiday spirit and enjoy indoor activities like visiting museums, theatres, and dining at cosy restaurants.

When planning your trip to New York City, consider what kind of weather and activities you prefer. Spring and fall offer mild temperatures and fewer crowds, making them ideal for outdoor exploration and sightseeing. Summer is perfect for those who enjoy warm weather and outdoor events, but be prepared for larger crowds and higher humidity. Winter, while cold, provides a unique opportunity to experience the city's holiday festivities and winter charm.

The best time to visit New York City depends on your personal preferences and the type of experience you're seeking. Each season has something special to offer, so no matter when you visit, you'll find plenty to see and do in this vibrant and dynamic city.

Visa Requirements and Essential Travel Documents

When planning a trip to New York City, understanding the visa requirements and ensuring you have all necessary travel documents is crucial. These steps help prevent any unexpected issues at the border, allowing you to focus on enjoying your visit.

For many travellers, obtaining a visa is a key part of the travel process. The United States has specific visa requirements based on your country of citizenship and the purpose of your visit. There are different types of visas, but for tourism purposes, the most common is the B-2 Tourist Visa. This visa is typically required for travellers from countries that do not participate in the Visa Waiver Program (VWP).

The Visa Waiver Program allows citizens from participating countries to visit the United States for up to 90 days without obtaining a visa. If your country is part of this program, you will need to apply for an Electronic System for Travel Authorisation (ESTA) before traveling. The ESTA is an online application that screens travellers and grants permission to enter the United States under the VWP. It is important to apply for ESTA well in advance of your trip to avoid any delays.

If you are from a country that does not participate in the VWP, or if your stay will exceed 90 days, you must apply for a B-2 Tourist Visa. This process usually involves completing an online application, paying a fee, and attending an interview at a U.S. embassy or consulate. During the interview, you may be asked to provide details about your trip, including your travel itinerary and financial means to support yourself during your stay. It is advisable to start this process several months before your planned departure date, as visa processing times can vary.

In addition to the visa, you will need a valid passport to enter the United States. Your passport must be valid for at least six months beyond your planned departure date from the United States. This requirement ensures that your passport does not expire while you are in the country. If your passport is due to expire soon, it is wise to renew it before applying for a visa or ESTA.

Another important document to carry is your travel itinerary. This includes your flight information, accommodation details, and a general outline of your plans while in New York City. Having a clear itinerary can be helpful when going through customs and immigration, as it shows that you have a well-organised trip planned. It can also assist you in navigating the city once you arrive.

You should also consider carrying a photocopy of your passport and visa, or ESTA approval. In the event that your passport is lost or stolen, having a copy can expedite the process of obtaining a replacement and verifying your identity. Keep this copy in a separate location from your original documents to reduce the risk of losing both.

If you plan to drive in the United States, you may need an International Driving Permit (IDP), depending on your home country. While many countries' licenses are recognised in the U.S., an IDP serves as a translation of your license and can be useful when renting a car or dealing with law enforcement.

Credit cards are widely accepted in New York City, but it is also a good idea to carry some cash for small purchases or in situations where cards are not accepted. Make sure your credit card is enabled for international use, and inform your bank of your travel plans to avoid any issues with card transactions.

Before travelling, it is also advisable to check the U.S. Customs and Border Protection (CBP) website for any updates or changes to entry requirements, as these can change based on global events or new regulations. The CBP website provides detailed information on what you can and cannot bring into the United States, helping you avoid potential issues at customs.

Having the correct visa or ESTA, a valid passport, and all necessary travel documents is essential for a smooth entry into New York City. By ensuring that all your documents are in order and carrying additional items like travel insurance and copies of important papers, you can focus on enjoying your trip without worrying about administrative hurdles. Preparation is key to a hassle-free travel experience, allowing you to fully immerse yourself in all that New York City has to offer.

Travel Insurance

Travel insurance is an essential part of planning any trip, including your visit to New York City. It provides a safety net that protects you against unexpected events that could disrupt your travel plans or cause significant financial loss. Understanding the benefits of travel insurance and why it is necessary can help you make informed decisions and ensure that you are well-prepared for your journey.

One of the primary reasons to consider travel insurance is the protection it offers in case of medical emergencies. Healthcare in the United States can be expensive, and without insurance, you may find yourself facing high medical bills if you require treatment during your trip. Travel insurance can cover the costs of doctor visits, hospital stays, and even emergency medical evacuations if necessary. This means that if you fall ill or have an accident, you won't have to worry about the financial burden of receiving the care you need.

Another important aspect of travel insurance is coverage for trip cancellations or interruptions. Life is unpredictable, and sometimes unforeseen circumstances can force you to cancel or cut short your trip. This could be due to personal reasons, such as illness or a family emergency, or external factors like severe weather or political unrest. Travel insurance can reimburse you for non-refundable expenses, such as flight tickets, hotel bookings, and tours, if you need to cancel or shorten your trip. This helps you avoid losing the money you've invested in your travel plans and gives you peace of mind knowing that you're protected against unexpected disruptions.

Travel insurance also covers lost, stolen, or damaged baggage and personal belongings. Losing your luggage or having valuable items stolen while travelling can be a stressful and costly experience. With travel insurance, you can receive compensation for the replacement of lost or damaged items, including essentials like clothing, electronics, and travel documents. This ensures that you can continue your trip without major disruptions, even if something goes wrong with your belongings.

In addition to these key benefits, travel insurance often includes coverage for delays. Flights can be delayed or cancelled for various reasons, leaving you stranded at the airport or causing you to miss connections. Travel insurance can cover additional expenses incurred during these delays, such as meals, accommodation, and transportation, helping you manage the inconvenience without adding extra financial stress.

For those planning adventurous activities during their trip to New York City, such as biking, kayaking, or even certain types of tours, travel insurance can offer special coverage for injuries or accidents that occur during these activities. This is particularly important if you plan to engage in activities that carry a higher risk of injury.

Another consideration is legal assistance, which some travel insurance policies provide. If you encounter legal issues while travelling, such as liability claims or the need for legal representation, your travel insurance can help cover the associated costs. This type of coverage may be less commonly needed, but it can be invaluable in certain situations.

Travel insurance is also useful for covering the costs associated with evacuations. In rare cases where natural disasters, political unrest, or other crises occur, you may need to be evacuated from the area quickly and safely. Travel insurance can cover the costs of emergency transportation and ensure that you are moved to a safer location or back home without bearing the full expense yourself.

When purchasing travel insurance, it is important to carefully review the policy details to understand what is covered and any exclusions that may apply. Policies can vary widely, so selecting one that matches your needs and the nature of your trip is crucial. Some insurance providers offer customisable plans that allow you to add or remove coverage options based on your specific requirements.

Travel insurance is a critical component of a well-planned trip to New York City. It provides financial protection and peace of mind in the face of unexpected events, ensuring that you can focus on enjoying your trip without worrying about what might go wrong. By securing the right travel insurance, you are taking a proactive step to safeguard your health, finances, and overall travel experience.

Essential Packing Tips

Packing for a trip to New York City requires careful consideration to ensure you have everything you need for a comfortable and enjoyable visit. The city's diverse climate and bustling urban environment mean that thoughtful preparation can greatly enhance your experience. Understanding what to pack and why each item is important can help you avoid common pitfalls and ensure that you are well-prepared for your adventure.

One of the key factors to consider when packing is the time of year you will be visiting. New York City experiences a wide range of temperatures throughout the year, so it's important to pack clothing that matches the season. For example, if you are visiting during the colder months, bringing warm layers is essential. A good-quality coat, scarves, gloves, and hat will keep you comfortable as you explore the city's outdoor attractions. On the other hand, if you plan to visit during the summer, lightweight and breathable clothing is ideal. The city can get quite warm, especially during the peak of summer, so packing items that help you stay cool is crucial.

Footwear is another critical consideration. New York City is a place where walking is a major part of getting around. You will likely spend a significant amount of time on your feet, whether you are exploring Central Park, visiting museums, or simply strolling through the city's neighborhoods. Comfortable, supportive shoes are a must. Choosing footwear that you can wear for extended periods without discomfort will make a big difference in how much you enjoy your trip. It's also wise to bring a pair of shoes that are versatile and can be worn in a variety of settings, from casual outings to more formal occasions.

Layering is an effective strategy for dressing in New York City, particularly in the transitional seasons of spring and fall. The weather can be unpredictable, with temperatures fluctuating throughout the day. By layering your clothing, you can easily adjust to changing conditions. For example, starting with a light base layer, adding a sweater, and then topping it off with a jacket allows you to remove or add layers as needed. This approach ensures that you remain comfortable throughout the day, regardless of the weather.

In addition to clothing, packing the right accessories can enhance your comfort and convenience. A sturdy, spacious bag or backpack is useful for carrying your daily essentials as you move around the city. Items like a reusable water bottle, sunglasses, and hat can help protect you from the elements and keep you hydrated and comfortable as you explore. A portable charger is another valuable item to have, especially if you plan to use your smartphone frequently for navigation, photos, and staying connected. With so much to see and do in New York City, the last thing you want is to run out of battery when you need it most.

For those who plan to use public transportation, it's helpful to bring a small wallet or pouch specifically for carrying your MetroCard or contactless payment card, as well as some cash. This keeps your transit essentials easily accessible, saving you time and hassle when boarding buses or entering subway stations. While credit and debit cards are widely accepted, having some cash on hand for smaller purchases or in situations where cards are not accepted can be convenient.

When it comes to personal items, don't forget to pack your travel-sized toiletries. While many hotels provide basic toiletries, having your own preferred products can add a touch of comfort to your stay. Items such as shampoo, conditioner, soap, and lotion should be packed in containers that meet airline carry-on regulations if you plan to bring them in your hand luggage. It's also a good idea to pack any necessary medications, along with a basic first aid kit that includes bandages, pain relievers, and any other items you might need during your trip.

Electronics and gadgets are an integral part of travel today, so packing them carefully is important. Bringing a power adapter if you are travelling from a country with different electrical outlets will ensure that you can charge your devices without any issues. A camera is also a worthwhile addition to your packing list if you want to capture high-quality photos of your experiences, though many travellers rely on their smartphones for this purpose.

Travel documents are another essential component of your packing preparations. Your passport, visa (if required), travel insurance details, and copies of important documents should all be organised and stored in a secure but easily accessible place. It's wise to have both physical and digital copies of these documents as a backup in case of loss or theft. Keeping a small folder or envelope in your bag for these items can help you stay organised and ensure that you have everything you need when you need it.

Finally, consider packing items that will make your flight and travel time more comfortable. Noise-cancelling headphones, a neck pillow, and an e-reader or book can help pass the time during your journey to New York City. If you are sensitive to light or noise, an eye mask and earplugs can make it easier to rest during your flight or in your accommodation.

By carefully selecting and organising your packing list, you can ensure that you have everything you need for a comfortable and enjoyable trip to New York City. With the right clothing, accessories, and personal items, you'll be well-prepared to navigate the city and make the most of your visit. Thoughtful packing is an investment in your travel experience, allowing you to focus on exploring and enjoying all that New York City has to offer.

Essential Apps

When visiting New York City, having the right tools at your disposal can significantly enhance your experience. In today's connected world, apps have become indispensable for travellers, offering assistance with everything from navigation to finding the best places to eat. Downloading the right apps before you arrive in New York City can help you maximise your experience, save time, and avoid potential frustrations.

One of the most crucial aspects of visiting New York City is navigating its vast and complex layout. The city's grid system can be straightforward in certain areas, but the sheer scale of the city can be overwhelming, especially for first-time visitors. This is where a reliable navigation app like **Google Maps** becomes invaluable. Google Maps provides real-time directions, detailed maps, and multiple transportation options, including walking, driving, and public transit. It also shows the quickest routes, estimated travel times, and even the best ways to avoid traffic or crowded areas. With Google Maps, you can explore the city with confidence, knowing that you'll always be on the right path.

Understanding the public transportation system in New York City is another key factor for a successful trip. The subway, buses, and other forms of public transit are widely used by locals and visitors alike, but they can be confusing for those unfamiliar with them. **Citymapper** is an app dedicated to simplifying public transportation in New York City. It provides real-time updates on subway schedules, bus routes, and service changes, helping you plan your journeys with precision. Citymapper includes features like detailed subway maps, fare calculators, and alerts for delays or disruptions, ensuring that you always know the best way to get where you're going.

Food is a major part of the New York City experience, and finding the best places to eat can be a highlight of your trip. The city offers a diverse culinary scene, ranging from street food to fine dining, and knowing where to go can make your visit even more memorable. **Yelp** is an excellent app for restaurants, reading reviews, and even making reservations at popular spots. Yelp provides menus, price ranges, and user-generated photos, allowing you to get a sense of what to expect before you arrive.

Staying connected while on the move is essential, and managing your data usage can be a challenge when traveling. **Maps.me** is a navigation app with offline capabilities, allowing you to access maps, directions, and other critical information without needing an active internet connection. This feature is particularly useful if you want to avoid roaming charges or if you find yourself in areas with poor reception. By downloading maps in advance, you can ensure that you always have access to the tools you need, regardless of your connectivity.

In a city as busy as New York, finding your way around can sometimes be stressful. That's why having an app that helps you locate essential services and amenities is a smart choice. **AroundMe** is an app that directs you to the nearest ATMs, restrooms, pharmacies, or convenience stores, ensuring that you can take care of your needs without unnecessary hassle. It can also point you towards nearby attractions, parks, and points of interest that you might otherwise miss, helping you make the most of your time in the city.

Another important aspect of your trip is keeping track of your expenses. Travelling in New York City can be expensive, and it's easy to lose track of your spending. **Trail Wallet** is a budgeting and expense tracking app designed specifically for travelers. By recording your expenses as you go, you can stay within your budget and avoid any surprises at the end of your trip. Trail Wallet allows you to categorise your spending, set limits, and even receive alerts if you're approaching your budget, ensuring that you can enjoy your trip without worrying about overspending.

Language barriers can sometimes be a concern for international visitors, and while English is the primary language spoken in New York City, you might find yourself in situations where communication is challenging. **Google Translate** is an app that can help bridge the gap, allowing you to communicate more easily with locals, read signs, and understand menus. Google Translate can translate text, voice, and even images in real-time, making it easier to navigate the city and interact with others.

Finally, one of the joys of visiting New York City is capturing memories of your trip. **Snapseed** is a great photo editing app that helps you enhance and share your photos. Snapseed offers tools to improve the quality of your photos, apply filters, and share your experiences with friends and family. It also includes features for creating photo albums or collages, allowing you to compile your memories in creative ways and cherish them long after your trip.

By equipping yourself with these essential apps, you can navigate New York City with greater ease, make informed decisions, and fully immerse yourself in the vibrant life of the city. These digital tools are like having a personal guide in your pocket, ready to assist you whenever you need it. With a little preparation and the right apps on your device, your trip to New York City will be as seamless and enjoyable as possible.

Cultural Etiquette and Local Customs

When visiting New York City, it is important to be aware of the local cultural etiquette and customs that shape daily interactions. This knowledge can help you navigate the city with ease and ensure that your experiences are positive and respectful. New York City is a vibrant and diverse place where people from all over the world live, work, and visit. Understanding the nuances of behaviour and expectations in this bustling environment can enhance your trip and help you connect more meaningfully with the city and its residents.

One of the most noticeable aspects of New York City culture is the fast pace of life. The city is known for its hustle and energy, and this is reflected in how people move and interact. Whether walking down the street, using public transportation, or engaging in daily activities, New Yorkers tend to be focused and direct. This sense of urgency can sometimes come across as impatience, but it is simply part of the city's rhythm. When navigating the streets or using the subway, it is important to keep up with the flow, stay aware of your surroundings, and avoid blocking pathways, especially in crowded areas.

Politeness and respect for personal space are also key components of local etiquette. While New Yorkers are often in a hurry, they value politeness and appreciate basic courtesies. Saying "please," "thank you," and "excuse me" can go a long way in making interactions smoother. Holding doors for others, offering a seat to someone in need on public transportation, and respecting lines are all common practices. Even though the city may seem fast-paced, small acts of kindness and consideration are noticed and appreciated.

New York City is a melting pot of cultures, and this diversity is reflected in the way people interact. It is common to encounter a wide range of languages, customs, and traditions as you move through different neighborhoods. This diversity is celebrated, and it is important to approach it with openness and respect. Being mindful of cultural differences and showing interest in the various communities within the city can enrich your experience. Avoid making assumptions about people based on their appearance or background, and be willing to learn from the different cultures you encounter.

Tipping is an important aspect of social etiquette in New York City. It is customary to tip service workers such as waitstaff, taxi drivers, and hotel staff as a gesture of appreciation for their service. In restaurants, a tip of around 15-20% of the total bill is standard, while tipping taxi drivers about 10-15% of the fare is typical. Hotel staff, such as bellhops and housekeeping, also appreciate tips for their services. Tipping is seen as a way to acknowledge the hard work of service industry workers, and it is common practice throughout the city.

When engaging in conversations, New Yorkers are known for their directness. This straightforward communication style may seem blunt to some, but it is not meant to be rude. Rather, it reflects a desire to get to the point and respect each other's time. Honesty and clarity are valued, and small talk is often brief. However, this does not mean that people are unfriendly. New Yorkers are generally open to helping visitors with directions or recommendations, and they appreciate it when visitors are clear about their needs or questions.

In social settings, punctuality is appreciated. Arriving on time for meetings, reservations, or events shows respect for other people's time. If you are running late, it is courteous to inform the person you are meeting as soon as possible. Being mindful of time, especially in a city where schedules are often tight, is a way to demonstrate consideration for others.

Public transportation is a central part of life in New York City, and there are certain unwritten rules that help keep things running smoothly. On the subway, it is polite to give up your seat for the elderly, pregnant women, or those with disabilities. Keeping your voice down and avoiding loud conversations or phone calls helps maintain a peaceful environment for everyone. When boarding or exiting trains, it is courteous to allow passengers to exit before entering and to stand clear of the doors to avoid blocking others.

Finally, New Yorkers take great pride in their city, and this pride is reflected in how they treat their surroundings. Keeping public spaces clean, disposing of trash properly, and respecting public property are important aspects of local etiquette. Whether you are visiting a park, a museum, or simply walking down the street, taking care of the environment and being mindful of your impact shows respect for the city and its residents.

By understanding and practicing these aspects of cultural etiquette and local customs, you can navigate New York City with confidence and enjoy a more fulfilling experience. Being aware of the city's unique pace, respecting personal space, embracing diversity, and following social norms will help you connect with the city on a deeper level. These small gestures of respect and consideration contribute to the vibrant, dynamic, and welcoming atmosphere that makes New York City such a remarkable place to visit.

Essential Safety Tips

When visiting New York City, being mindful of safety is important to ensure that your trip is enjoyable and free from unnecessary worries. While New York City is generally safe for tourists, it is still a large urban area with its own set of challenges. Understanding how to navigate the city safely can help you make the most of your visit and avoid potential risks.

One of the most basic principles of staying safe in New York City is being aware of your surroundings. The city is bustling with activity, and it's easy to become distracted by the sights and sounds. However, staying alert to what's happening around you is key to avoiding problems. When walking down the street, keep an eye on your belongings and be cautious of your surroundings, especially in crowded areas like Times Square or during events where large crowds gather. Pickpocketing can occur in busy locations, so keeping your personal items secure and close to your body is advisable.

Using public transportation is a common and efficient way to get around New York City, but it also requires some attention to safety. When using the subway, it's important to stay within well-lit and populated areas, particularly during the evening or at night. Avoid empty subway cars, and choose one that has other passengers. On platforms, stand back from the edge and wait for the train at a safe distance. If you ever feel uncomfortable, move to a different car or wait for the next train. Being aware of your environment and following these simple guidelines can make your subway experience smoother and safer.

Another safety consideration is how you manage your money and valuables. Carrying large amounts of cash is not recommended; instead, use credit or debit cards for most transactions. If you need to withdraw cash, use ATMs located inside banks or well-populated areas rather than those on the street. When handling your money, do so discreetly to avoid drawing attention. It's also a good idea to keep your wallet in a secure, less accessible place, such as an inside pocket, to reduce the risk of theft.

New York City is home to many world-famous attractions, but it's also a place where scams and fraudulent activities can occur. Being aware of common scams can help you avoid falling victim to them. For example, some individuals may approach you offering fake tickets to events or attractions at discounted prices. To avoid being scammed, only purchase tickets from official sources, such as the venue's box office or authorised ticket sellers. Additionally, be cautious of anyone who tries to pressure you into making quick decisions or asks for personal information.

When it comes to navigating the streets, staying safe is also about being mindful of traffic. New York City is known for its busy streets and fast-paced drivers. When crossing the street, always use designated crosswalks and follow pedestrian signals. Even when you have the right of way, it's important to look both ways and ensure that oncoming vehicles are stopping before you cross. Many accidents can be avoided by simply being cautious and not rushing across the street.

If you decide to explore the city's nightlife, it's important to do so with safety in mind. Stick to well-known establishments, and if you're unfamiliar with an area, it's a good idea to research it beforehand. If you're going out at night, consider using a rideshare service or a licensed taxi to get to and from your destination. Walking alone at night in unfamiliar or less populated areas is not advisable. When enjoying drinks, be mindful of how much you consume, and never leave your drink unattended.

Another tip for staying safe in New York City is to keep a charged phone with you at all times. This ensures that you can call for help if needed or use navigation apps to find your way. It's also helpful to have a backup portable charger, especially if you're out exploring for long periods. Make sure you have important contacts saved in your phone, including local emergency numbers and the contact information for your hotel.

In case of an emergency, knowing how to reach help quickly is essential. Familiarise yourself with the location of the nearest police stations, hospitals, or tourist help centres in the areas you plan to visit. If you find yourself in an emergency situation, don't hesitate to call 911, the emergency services number in the United States, which can connect you with police, fire, or medical assistance.

Finally, respecting local laws and customs contributes to your safety and helps you avoid unnecessary trouble. Understanding local regulations, such as those related to alcohol consumption, smoking, and public behaviour, will help you stay within the boundaries of the law and enjoy a hassle-free visit. If you're ever unsure about something, asking a local or doing a quick search can clarify the rules and keep you on the right track.

By following these safety tips, you can confidently explore New York City while minimising risks. Staying alert, being prepared, and exercising caution will allow you to enjoy everything the city has to offer without compromising your safety. New York City is a place full of exciting opportunities, and by taking the right precautions, you can ensure that your visit is both safe and memorable.

As you prepare for your trip to New York City, taking the time to plan ahead will help you make the most of your visit. By understanding the essentials, you'll be ready to enjoy everything the city has to offer with confidence. With a little preparation, your experience in New York City will be smooth, enjoyable, and filled with unforgettable moments.

CHAPTER 2

Neighbourhoods

New York City is a city of diverse neighborhoods. Each area has its own vibe, shaped by the people who live there, the history behind it, and the unique spots that make it stand out. The city is made up of five distinct boroughs, each with its own unique neighbourhood.

Manhattan

Scan the QR code to see the map of Manhattan

Manhattan is the iconic heart of New York City, where you'll find towering skyscrapers and historic streets. This borough is home to some of the most famous landmarks in the world and offers a lot in respect to culture, commerce, and history.

Neighbourhoods here include: Wall Street, Harlem, SoHo, Greenwich Village.

Getting There

From JFK Airport

Take the AirTrain to Jamaica Station, then transfer to the E subway line to reach Midtown Manhattan. From there, the subway can take you to other neighbourhoods.

From Newark Airport

The AirTrain connects you to NJ Transit, which brings you into Penn Station in Manhattan. Subways or taxis can take you further.

From LaGuardia Airport

The Q70 bus connects to the subway system at Roosevelt Avenue, providing access to various Manhattan neighbourhoods.

Attractions

Statue of Liberty

Central Park

Empire State Building

Times Square

Broadway

Accommodation Options

Solo Travellers

Pod 51 Hotel

Couples

The Library Hotel

Families

The Beacon Hotel

Groups

Marriott Marquis

Transportation

The subway is the most efficient way to navigate Manhattan, with lines covering the entire borough. Walking is also a great way to explore the city's streets, especially in neighbourhoods like SoHo and Greenwich Village.

Recommended Restaurants

Joe's Pizza

The River Café

Ellen's Stardust Diner

Carmine's

Brooklyn

Scan the QR code to see the map of Brooklyn

Brooklyn is where New York's creative energy thrives, offering hip neighbourhoods, historic sites, and stunning views of the Manhattan skyline.

Neighbourhoods here include: Williamsburg, DUMBO, Brooklyn Heights, Park Slope.

Getting There

From JFK Airport

Take the AirTrain to Howard Beach, then transfer to the A subway line to reach various parts of Brooklyn.

From Newark Airport

Use NJ Transit to reach Manhattan, then transfer to subway lines like the L or A to get into Brooklyn.

From LaGuardia Airport

The Q70 bus to Jackson Heights connects you to subway lines that lead directly to Brooklyn.

Attractions

Brooklyn Bridge

Prospect Park

Coney Island

Brooklyn Museum

Barclays Centre

Accommodation Options

Solo Travellers

The Williamsburg Hotel

Couples

1 Hotel Brooklyn Bridge

Families

Hotel Le Bleu

Groups

The Box House Hotel

Transportation

Brooklyn's neighbourhoods are well-connected by subway lines like the L, A, and F. Buses are also available, and walking around neighbourhoods like DUMBO and Williamsburg is a great way to soak in the local atmosphere.

Recommended Restaurants

Juliana's Pizza

The River Café

Brooklyn Farmacy & Soda Fountain

Roberta's

Queens

Scan the QR code to see the map of Queens

Queens is the most ethnically diverse borough in New York City.

Neighbourhoods here include: Astoria, Flushing, Long Island City, Jackson Heights.

Getting There

From JFK Airport

Use the AirTrain to connect with the E or A subway lines, which run through several key neighbourhoods in Queens.

From Newark Airport

NJ Transit to Manhattan, then transfer to lines like the 7 to reach Queens.

From LaGuardia Airport

The Q70 bus connects directly to Roosevelt Avenue, a major hub for Queens-bound subway lines.

Attractions

Flushing Meadows-Corona Park

Museum of the Moving Image

MoMA PS1

Queens Botanical Garden

Gantry Plaza State Park

Accommodation Options

Solo Travellers

The Paper Factory Hotel

Couples

Boro Hotel

Families

The Parc Hotel

Groups

The Local NYC

Transportation

Queens is served by multiple subway lines, including the 7, E, and F trains. Buses are also widely available, and certain neighbourhoods are easily explored by foot. The borough's expansive layout means that public transportation is the best way to get around.

Recommended Restaurants

Xi'an Famous Foods

Tournesol

Jackson Diner

Taverna Kyclades

The Bronx

Scan the QR code to see the map of Bronx

The Bronx is a borough rich in history and culture, known for its iconic Yankee Stadium, beautiful parks, and vibrant arts scene.

Neighbourhoods here include: Riverdale, Belmont (Arthur Avenue, often referred to as the "Real Little Italy" of New York), South Bronx, Fordham.

Getting There

From JFK Airport

Take the AirTrain to Jamaica Station, then transfer to the E or A line to Manhattan. From there, transfer to the 4 or D subway lines, which run through the Brooklyn.

From Newark Airport

NJ Transit to Manhattan, then use the subway system to reach the Bronx, particularly the 4, B, or D lines.

From LaGuardia Airport

The M60 bus connects to the subway in Manhattan, where you can transfer to Bronx-bound lines.

Attractions

Yankee Stadium

Bronx Zoo

New York Botanical Garden

Wave Hill

Arthur Avenue (Belmont)

Accommodation Options

Solo Travellers

Opera House Hotel

Couples

Edge Hotel

Families

Residence Inn by Marriott

Groups

The Bronx Guesthouse

Transportation

The Bronx is well-served by the 4, B, and D subway lines, which connect to various neighbourhoods and attractions. Buses are also a convenient option for getting around within the borough. Walking is ideal in areas like Arthur Avenue, where you can explore local shops and eateries.

Recommended Restaurants

Dominick's

Havana Café

Zero Otto Nove

City Island Lobster House

Staten Island

Scan the QR code to see the map of Staten Island

Staten Island offers a different pace from the rest of New York City, with its parks, beaches, and charming small-town feel. It's the ideal destination for those looking to enjoy some peaceful exploration.

Neighbourhoods here include: St. George, Tottenville, Great Kills, Richmond Town.

Getting There

From JFK Airport

AirTrain to Jamaica Station, then the E subway line to Manhattan. From there, transfer to the Staten Island Ferry at the Whitehall Terminal.

From Newark Airport

Use NJ Transit to Manhattan, then the 1 or R subway lines to South Ferry for the Staten Island Ferry.

From LaGuardia Airport

The Q70 bus connects to Roosevelt Avenue, where you can transfer to the subway system leading to the Staten Island Ferry.

Attractions

Staten Island Ferry

Snug Harbour Cultural Centre & Botanical Garden

Staten Island Zoo

Historic Richmond Town

Great Kills Park

Accommodation Options

Solo Travellers

The Harbour House

Couples

Victorian Bed & Breakfast of Staten Island

Families

Hampton Inn & Suites

Groups

Fairfield Inn & Suites

Transportation

Staten Island is most easily accessed via the Staten Island Ferry, a free service that provides stunning views of the Statue of Liberty and Manhattan skyline. Once on the island, local buses and the Staten Island Railway are available to get around. For exploring the more remote areas, renting a car is a practical option.

Recommended Restaurants

Enoteca Maria

Blue

Ralph's Famous Italian Ices

Denino's Pizzeria & Tavern

New York City's neighbourhoods all have a lot to offer, and exploring them is one of the most rewarding parts of any visit. These areas are what give the city its character. By venturing into different neighbourhoods, you'll get a real sense of what makes this city so diverse and full of life. Each place you explore will leave a lasting impression, showing you just how much New York City has to offer.

CHAPTER 3

Transportation

Getting to and around New York City can seem overwhelming at first, with its vast network of streets, subways, and buses. However, once you understand the basics, navigating the city becomes much easier. Efficient transportation is key to making the most of your time here. You'll get to know the best ways to travel to and within the city, helping you get from place to place smoothly and enjoyably.

Getting There

New York City is one of the most accessible cities in the world, drawing visitors from all corners of the globe. However you're arriving, understanding the best ways to reach the city is crucial for a smooth start to your trip. The city's transportation infrastructure is extensive, designed to accommodate millions of visitors each year. Knowing how to navigate these options can make your arrival stress-free and set the tone for a successful visit.

If you're flying into New York City, there are three major airports that serve the metropolitan area: John F. Kennedy International Airport (JFK), Newark Liberty International Airport (EWR), and LaGuardia Airport (LGA). Each airport offers different advantages depending on where you're coming from and where you're headed in the city.

John F. Kennedy International Airport, located in Queens, is one of the busiest airports in the United States. It handles the majority of international flights into New York City. JFK is well-connected to the city via various transportation options, making it easy to get to your final destination. If you're heading to Manhattan or other parts of the city, you can use the AirTrain service, which links the airport terminals with the subway and the Long Island Rail Road (LIRR). From there, you can take a subway or train into the heart of the city. Taxis, rideshares, and shuttle services are also readily available outside each terminal, offering a more direct route to your destination.

Newark Liberty International Airport is located in New Jersey, just across the Hudson River from Manhattan. Despite being in a different state, Newark is a popular choice for travellers heading to New York City, particularly those arriving from international destinations or the West Coast. Like JFK, Newark is connected to the city via the AirTrain, which links to NJ Transit and Amtrak services. These trains take you directly to Penn Station in Manhattan, making it a convenient option for those staying in Midtown or Downtown. Additionally, taxis and rideshare services are available for a more straightforward journey to your accommodation.

LaGuardia Airport, also located in Queens, is the closest airport to Manhattan, making it a preferred choice for domestic travelers. Although LaGuardia does not have a direct train connection to the city, it is well served by buses that connect to the subway system. The M60 bus, for instance, takes you directly from LaGuardia to various points in Manhattan, where you can transfer to the subway. Taxis and rideshare services are also a quick and convenient way to get into the city from LaGuardia, often providing the fastest route to your destination.

For those arriving by train, Penn Station and Grand Central Terminal are the primary rail hubs in New York City. Penn Station, located in Midtown Manhattan, is the busiest train station in the country, serving Amtrak, NJ Transit, and Long Island RailRoad passengers. It is a central point for those travelling from other cities in the Northeast Corridor, such as Washington, D.C., Philadelphia, and Boston. Grand Central Terminal, also in Midtown, primarily serves the Metro-North Railroad, which connects New York City with the northern suburbs and parts of Connecticut. Both stations are well integrated with the city's subway system, making it easy to continue your journey once you arrive.

If you're driving to New York City, it's important to be aware that the city's traffic can be challenging, especially during peak hours. Major highways like Interstate 95 and the New Jersey Turnpike feed into the city, leading to various bridges and tunnels that connect to Manhattan. The George Washington Bridge, Lincoln Tunnel, and Holland Tunnel are key entry points from the west, while the Queens-Midtown Tunnel and Brooklyn-Battery Tunnel provide access from other parts of the city. Parking in Manhattan can be expensive and scarce, so it's often best to park outside the city and use public transportation to get around.

For those preferring to travel by bus, New York City is a major hub for several long-distance bus services. The Port Authority Bus Terminal in Midtown Manhattan is the main arrival point for buses coming from cities across the East Coast and beyond. Companies like Greyhound, Megabus, and BoltBus offer frequent services to and from New York City, providing a cost-effective option for travelers. Once at the terminal, you can easily access the subway or hail a taxi to reach your final destination.

Regardless of how you arrive, having a clear plan for getting to your accommodation from your point of entry will make the start of your trip much smoother. Understanding the available transportation options ensures that you can navigate the city efficiently from the moment you arrive. By planning ahead, you can avoid the common pitfalls of navigating a new city and instead focus on enjoying all that New York has to offer.

Getting Around

Navigating New York City can seem overwhelming at first, but with a little knowledge, it becomes much more manageable. The city offers a range of ways to get from one place to another, each with its own advantages. Understanding how to move efficiently through the city's busy streets and neighbourhoods is key to making the most of your time here. This section will guide you through the best ways to get around, helping you explore the city with ease.

The Subway System

The New York City subway system is one of the most essential and efficient ways to travel across the city. It is an expansive network that covers the boroughs of Manhattan, Brooklyn, Queens, and the Bronx, offering a reliable means of transportation to millions of people daily. While it may seem overwhelming at first glance, understanding how the subway works can greatly simplify your travels and make getting around the city a breeze.

The subway operates 24 hours a day, seven days a week, making it a convenient option no matter the time of day. The network consists of numerous lines, each identified by either a letter or a number, and each line is colour-coded on the subway map. These lines run along various routes, covering the entire city and connecting major neighbourhoods, landmarks, and points of interest. The trains themselves are also labelled with the corresponding letter or number of the line, making it easy to identify the correct train to board.

Stations are spread throughout the city, with some intersections serving multiple lines. When entering a station, you may find that different entrances lead to different platforms depending on the direction of travel—uptown, downtown, or crosstown. It is important to pay attention to the signs indicating which trains stop at each platform and in which direction they are heading. This will help you avoid getting on a train going in the wrong direction.

Each subway line typically runs on two tracks, one for each direction, but some lines share tracks with other lines, especially in busy areas like Midtown Manhattan. This means that more than one train line may stop at the same platform, so it's essential to listen to announcements and check the train's display to ensure you are boarding the correct one. Most trains have digital displays and automated announcements that indicate the next stop and final destination, providing real-time updates that help passengers stay informed.

Fares for the subway are consistent across the system, and payment is made using a MetroCard or contactless payment methods, such as a smartphone or contactless credit card. MetroCards can be purchased and reloaded at vending machines located in every station. They are available as pay-per-ride or unlimited ride options, with the latter being more economical if you plan to use the subway frequently during your stay. Once you have your MetroCard or contactless payment method ready, simply swipe or tap it at the turnstile to gain entry to the subway platform.

One of the key aspects of understanding the subway system is familiarising yourself with the difference between local and express trains. Local trains stop at every station along their route, making them ideal for short trips within a specific neighbourhood or for reaching less frequently serviced stations. Express trains, on the other hand, skip certain stations and only stop at major hubs, allowing for quicker travel across longer distances. These express services are particularly useful when travelling between boroughs or covering more significant portions of the city.

To make your journey smoother, it's also important to understand the concept of "transfers" within the subway system. A transfer allows you to switch from one train line to another without exiting the station or paying an additional fare. Transfer points are clearly marked on subway maps and in the stations themselves. Knowing where and how to transfer can save you time and help you reach your destination more efficiently.

While the subway system is generally reliable, delays and service changes can occur, especially during weekends or late-night hours when maintenance work is often carried out. It's a good practice to check for any service updates before heading out. These updates are available on the Metropolitan Transportation Authority (MTA) website, on transportation apps, and often posted at stations. If you encounter a delay or service disruption, the MTA usually provides alternative routes or shuttle buses to help you reach your destination.

Safety is another consideration when using the subway. While the system is generally safe, especially during the day, it's always a good idea to remain aware of your surroundings. Keep your belongings secure and within sight, and try to stay in well-lit, populated areas of the station, particularly if travelling at night. Many stations have security cameras, and there are MTA employees and police officers on duty to assist with any concerns.

For those new to the subway system, using a map is essential. Subway maps are available at most stations, and digital versions are accessible through various apps and websites. The map not only helps you plan your route but also gives you a sense of where you are in relation to the rest of the city. It's beneficial to take a moment to study the map before starting your journey, as it can help prevent confusion and ensure that you take the most efficient route to your destination.

Mastering the New York City subway system opens up a world of possibilities for exploring the city. While it may appear complex at first, with a little practice and attention to detail, you'll find that it's one of the most effective and affordable ways to get around. By understanding the basics of how the system works, from reading the maps to knowing how to transfer, you can confidently navigate the city and make the most of your time in New York.

Buses

Navigating New York City can be a complex task, but the city's extensive bus system offers a practical and accessible way to get around. While the subway is often the first choice for many travellers, buses provide a valuable alternative, particularly for shorter trips, crosstown travel, and reaching destinations not served by the subway. Understanding the bus routes can greatly enhance your ability to explore the city efficiently and comfortably.

The bus system in New York City is operated by the Metropolitan Transportation Authority (MTA), which also manages the subway. Buses cover all five boroughs (Manhattan, Brooklyn, Queens, the Bronx, and Staten Island), ensuring that even the more remote or less frequently visited areas are accessible. Each bus route is identified by a combination of a letter and number, which indicates the borough it primarily serves. For example, buses in Manhattan often begin with "M," while those in Queens start with "Q." These identifiers help passengers quickly recognise the buses serving their specific area.

One of the significant advantages of using the bus system is the ability to see the city as you travel. Unlike the subway, which runs underground for much of its route, buses provide views of the neighbourhoods, streets, and landmarks as you move from one place to another. This makes bus travel not just a practical option but also an opportunity to experience the city from a different perspective. For visitors who prefer to avoid the crowded and often hectic atmosphere of the subway, buses offer a more relaxed and scenic alternative.

Buses in New York City operate on a regular schedule, with frequent service during peak hours and reduced service late at night. Bus stops are clearly marked with signs that display the route number and the direction the bus is heading. Many bus stops also include a route map and a list of key stops along the way. When waiting for a bus, it's important to stand at the designated bus stop to ensure the driver sees you and stops. Boarding is typically done at the front of the bus, where passengers can pay their fare using a MetroCard or a contactless payment option.

Once aboard, the fare system on buses is straightforward. The same MetroCard used for the subway can be used on buses, and transfers between buses or from the subway to a bus (and vice versa) are generally free within a two-hour window. This makes it easy to switch between different modes of transport as you navigate the city. Buses also accommodate those with mobility issues, offering wheelchair-accessible features like ramps and designated seating areas.

For crosstown travel, especially in Manhattan, buses can be more convenient than the subway. Crosstown buses run across the city from east to west (and vice versa), providing direct access to areas that might require several subway transfers. These routes are particularly useful for reaching places like Central Park, the Metropolitan Museum of Art, or the American Museum of Natural History. Understanding which crosstown routes serve your destinations can save time and simplify your travel plans.

In addition to regular buses, New York City offers Select Bus Service (SBS), which operates on specific high-traffic routes. SBS is designed to reduce travel times by incorporating features like off-board fare payment, which allows passengers to pay before boarding and board the bus through any door. SBS buses are also equipped with dedicated lanes in some areas, reducing the impact of traffic and ensuring a quicker, more efficient ride. For busy routes where time is of the essence, SBS provides a faster and more convenient option.

By familiarising yourself with the routes and services available, you can make informed decisions and enjoy all that New York City has to offer, no matter where your journey takes you.

Taxis, Rideshares and Private Transport

Navigating NYC can be a complex experience, especially when considering the many transportation options available. Among these, taxis, rideshares, and private transport offer convenient and flexible ways to get around the city. Each of these options provides unique benefits depending on your specific needs, whether you're looking for a quick ride across town, a comfortable journey with luggage, or a private transfer to and from the airport. Understanding how to utilise these services effectively will ensure that your travels within the city are smooth and hassle-free.

Taxis have long been a symbol of New York City, with their iconic yellow cabs visible throughout the streets of Manhattan and beyond. Hailing a taxi is a simple and straightforward process. You can find taxis almost anywhere in the city, and in many areas, especially in Manhattan, it's as easy as raising your hand at the curb. Once you're inside the cab, the fare is calculated based on the distance travelled and the time spent in traffic. Taxis are equipped with meters that clearly display the fare, and payments can be made in cash or by credit card. Taxis are a reliable option for short trips, late-night travel, or when you need a direct route to your destination.

For those seeking more control over their transportation, rideshare services like Uber and Lyft offer a flexible and convenient alternative. These services allow you to book a ride directly from your smartphone, providing real-time information on the estimated fare, the time of arrival, and the driver's details. This can be particularly helpful in areas where taxis may be less available or during peak hours when demand is high. Rideshares also offer a range of vehicle options, from standard cars to luxury vehicles, depending on your preferences and needs. The app-based system means that you can track your ride's progress, communicate with your driver, and even split fares with other passengers if you're travelling with friends or colleagues.

In addition to taxis and rideshares, private transport services are another option for those looking for a more personalised experience. Private car services, often referred to as black car services, provide professional drivers and vehicles that can be booked in advance for specific times and locations. These services are particularly useful for airport transfers, business travel, or special occasions where punctuality and comfort are essential. Private transport companies offer a variety of vehicles, including sedans, SUVs, and even limousines, catering to different group sizes and preferences. The cost of private transport is typically higher than that of taxis or rideshares, but the benefits of having a dedicated driver and a more tailored service can be well worth the expense.

One of the advantages of using taxis, rideshares, or private transport in New York City is the ability to reach destinations that may not be as accessible by public transportation. While the subway and bus systems cover a vast area, there are still places in the city that require a bit more effort to reach, such as certain neighbourhoods in the outer boroughs or areas that are off the main transit lines. In these cases, a taxi, rideshare, or private car can provide a direct route, saving you time and ensuring that you arrive exactly where you need to be.

When considering which option to choose, it's important to think about factors such as cost, convenience, and the specifics of your journey. Taxis are generally more affordable for short distances, while rideshares offer flexibility in terms of vehicle choice and the ability to plan and pay for your ride ahead of time. Private transport is ideal for those who require a higher level of service, such as a meet-and-greet at the airport or a chauffeured experience for a special event.

Safety is a key consideration when using any form of transport, and both taxis and rideshares in New York City are regulated to ensure the safety of passengers. Taxis are licensed by the city and must adhere to strict safety and service standards, including regular inspections and background checks for drivers. Rideshare companies also perform background checks on their drivers and offer features such as GPS tracking and driver ratings to help ensure a safe ride. Private transport services, often used by corporate clients and high-profile individuals, are typically operated by professional drivers who are trained to provide a high level of service.

For those unfamiliar with the city, taxis and rideshares offer the added benefit of having a local driver who knows the area well. Whether you're heading to a popular tourist destination or a hidden gem in one of the city's many neighbourhoods, your driver can navigate the streets efficiently, avoiding traffic and ensuring that you reach your destination as quickly as possible. Additionally, the familiarity of a driver with local traffic patterns and road conditions can make your journey more comfortable and less stressful, particularly during peak traffic times.

Taxis, rideshares, and private transport each provide valuable options for getting around New York City. By understanding the advantages of each, you can choose the best method of transportation for your specific needs.

Bikes and Scooters

New York City is a place of constant movement, with its streets always bustling with people, cars, and buses. However, one of the most engaging and flexible ways to explore the city is on a bike or scooter. These modes of transportation offer a unique perspective on the city, allowing you to navigate its neighbourhoods, parks, and waterfronts at your own pace.

Biking in New York City has become increasingly popular over the years, thanks to the city's investment in bike lanes, paths, and bike-sharing programs. Cycling allows you to cover more ground than walking while still giving you the freedom to stop and explore whenever something catches your eye. The city's grid layout, especially in Manhattan, makes navigation relatively straightforward, and with dedicated bike lanes on many major streets, biking is both a practical and enjoyable way to get around.

Citi Bike, New York City's bike-sharing program, is one of the easiest ways to rent a bike for short trips. With thousands of bikes available at docking stations throughout the city, Citi Bike provides a convenient option for both residents and visitors. You can pick up a bike at one station and drop it off at another, making it perfect for one-way trips or commuting between attractions. The bikes are designed to be durable and easy to use, with adjustable seats and simple gearing. To access a bike, you can purchase a single ride, day pass, or membership through the Citi Bike app or at a docking station kiosk.

When biking in New York City, it's important to be aware of the traffic and to follow the rules of the road. While the city has made significant strides in improving bike safety, the streets can still be busy and sometimes chaotic. Riding in a bike lane is recommended whenever possible, as it provides a designated space separated from car traffic. In areas without bike lanes, cyclists should ride with the flow of traffic, staying to the right and being cautious at intersections. Wearing a helmet is strongly advised, as it significantly reduces the risk of injury in case of an accident.

New York City's parks are some of the best places to enjoy a bike ride. Central Park, for example, offers a scenic loop that takes you through its various landscapes, from open meadows to wooded areas. The Hudson River Greenway is another popular route, running along the west side of Manhattan with beautiful views of the river and New Jersey across the water. In Brooklyn, Prospect Park provides a similar experience with a car-free loop that's perfect for leisurely rides. These areas are not only safer for cyclists due to less traffic but also offer a chance to experience the natural beauty of the city.

Scooters have also become a popular transportation option in New York City, especially for short trips. While not as widely available as bikes, electric scooters can be a fun and efficient way to get around, particularly in areas where public transportation is less convenient. Some companies offer scooter rentals through apps, similar to bike-sharing programs. These scooters are electric, meaning they require minimal effort to ride, and can be particularly useful for getting around neighbourhoods or covering distances that might be too far to walk but too short for a subway ride.

When riding a scooter, many of the same rules that apply to biking also apply. It's important to ride in bike lanes or on the street rather than on sidewalks to avoid conflicts with pedestrians. Scooter riders should also be mindful of their speed, particularly in crowded areas, and should always be on the lookout for cars, especially when crossing intersections. Just like with biking, wearing a helmet is recommended for safety.

Both biking and riding scooters offer a degree of freedom and flexibility that other forms of transportation don't. You're not confined by schedules or routes, and you can explore parts of the city that might be difficult to reach by car or subway. These modes of transportation also allow you to engage more directly with the city's environment, whether it's feeling the breeze as you ride along the waterfront or stopping to check out a street performance in a local park.

Another benefit of using bikes or scooters is the ability to avoid some of the city's notorious traffic congestion. While cars and buses might get stuck in gridlock, cyclists and scooter riders can often make quicker progress, especially during peak traffic times. This can be particularly advantageous in areas like Midtown Manhattan, where traffic is heavy but bike lanes are available to provide a faster alternative.

For those concerned about the environment, biking and scootering are also eco-friendly transportation options. They produce no emissions, making them a great choice for those looking to reduce their carbon footprint while exploring the city. Additionally, the exercise involved in biking is a healthy way to stay active during your visit, offering a workout that's both enjoyable and functional.

Bikes and scooters provide a versatile and enjoyable way to experience New York City. By understanding the rules and best practices for biking and scootering in New York, you can ensure a safe, efficient, and memorable journey through one of the world's most dynamic cities.

Ferries

Exploring New York City by ferry offers a unique and refreshing way to see the city. The waterways that surround Manhattan, Brooklyn, Queens, and Staten Island are not just scenic backdrops but also provide vital transportation routes that connect various parts of the city. Using ferries to get around allows you to experience the city from a different perspective while also avoiding some of the congestion and delays associated with other modes of transportation.

Ferries in New York City serve both locals and visitors, offering routes that connect major neighbourhoods, business districts, and tourist attractions. The ferry system is an integral part of the city's transportation network, providing an alternative to the subway and buses, especially for those travelling between boroughs. One of the most iconic ferry services is the Staten Island Ferry, which operates between Staten Island and Lower Manhattan. This ferry is not only a crucial link for commuters but also a popular attraction for visitors, offering stunning views of the Statue of Liberty, Ellis Island, and the Manhattan skyline. The Staten Island Ferry is free to ride, making it an accessible and cost-effective way to see some of New York's most famous sights from the water.

In addition to the Staten Island Ferry, the NYC Ferry service offers a more extensive network of routes that connect various parts of the city. These ferries operate along the East River and provide connections between Manhattan, Brooklyn, Queens, and the Bronx. The routes are designed to make it easier to travel between waterfront neighbourhoods, with stops at key locations such as Wall Street, East 34th Street, and various piers in Brooklyn and Queens. Riding the NYC Ferry is a pleasant way to commute or explore, offering a relaxed atmosphere away from the hustle of the streets.

One of the advantages of using ferries to get around New York City is the opportunity to enjoy the city's waterfront. The views from the ferry are unmatched, offering panoramic vistas of the skyline, bridges, and landmarks that are often missed when travelling by car or subway. Whether you are crossing the East River, gliding past the towering buildings of Midtown Manhattan, or taking in the greenery of Governors Island, the ferry ride provides a moment of calm and beauty amidst the city's fast pace.

Ferries are also an efficient means of transportation for reaching areas that might be more difficult to access by other modes of transit. For example, the ferry routes connecting Manhattan with the Brooklyn neighbourhoods of DUMBO and Red Hook allow for quick and direct access to these areas, which are known for their vibrant arts scenes and historical significance. Similarly, ferries from Manhattan to the Rockaways in Queens offer a convenient way to reach the beaches, especially during the summer months when traffic to these areas can be heavy.

Using the ferry system is straightforward. Tickets for the NYC ferry can be purchased online, through a mobile app, or at kiosks located at the ferry terminals. The fare is affordable, and the experience of travelling by ferry is well worth it, considering the views and comfort it provides. The ferry terminals are equipped with waiting areas, and the ferries themselves offer seating both indoors and outdoors, catering to different preferences and weather conditions.

For those who are commuting or travelling with specific destinations in mind, the ferry service provides regular schedules with frequent departures throughout the day. This makes it easy to plan your trip and ensures that you won't have to wait long for the next ferry. The ferry operate year-round, although schedules may vary slightly depending on the season. It's always a good idea to check the current schedule before heading to the terminal to ensure that you are on time for your desired departure.

Safety on the ferries is a priority, with all vessels equipped with life jackets and other emergency equipment. The crew members are trained to handle a variety of situations, ensuring that passengers can enjoy their journey with peace of mind. The ferry terminals are also well-maintained, with clear signage and staff available to assist passengers with any questions or concerns.

Ferry rides are also a great option for those looking to incorporate a bit of sightseeing into their daily commute or leisure travel. The routes often pass by or near major landmarks, giving passengers the chance to take in the sights without the need for a dedicated tour. For example, the ferry ride from Manhattan to Staten Island provides close-up views of the Statue of Liberty and Ellis Island, offering a perspective that is both iconic and memorable.

For visitors and locals alike, ferries provide a chance to escape the intensity of the city streets and enjoy a peaceful journey across the water. The experience of travelling by ferry is different from that of other forms of transportation in New York City; it is more relaxed, offering a chance to take in the fresh air and enjoy the natural surroundings. Whether you are commuting to work, visiting friends in another borough, or simply looking for a new way to see the city, the ferry system offers an enjoyable and practical solution.

Getting around New York City by ferry is not only efficient but also offers a unique and enjoyable way to experience the city. The combination of convenience, scenic views, and the chance to explore waterfront neighbourhoods makes the ferry a valuable part of New York's transportation network.

Walking

Walking through New York City is one of the most immersive and rewarding ways to experience the city. The energy, diversity, and vibrancy of New York are best felt when you take to the streets, where every block offers something new and unexpected. From the towering skyscrapers of Manhattan to the charming brownstones of Brooklyn, walking allows you to connect with the city in a way that no other mode of transportation can match.

New York City is designed to be walked. The grid layout of Manhattan, with its numbered streets running east to west and avenues running north to south, makes navigation relatively simple. This grid system means that getting lost is less of a concern, and it's easy to calculate the distance between your starting point and destination. Each block is about a minute's walk, and the regularity of the grid helps you cover ground efficiently.

Walking in New York offers a closeness to the city's architecture, culture, and people that isn't possible from the seat of a car or even a bike. As you walk, you'll notice the small details that make each neighbourhood unique—the historic buildings, the bustling markets, the street art that adorns walls and alleyways. Walking gives you the freedom to stop and explore at your own pace, whether you're drawn to a cosy café, an art gallery, or a hidden park.

The scale of New York City's neighbourhoods also makes walking practical. Many of the city's most famous attractions are within walking distance of each other, especially in areas like Midtown Manhattan. You can easily spend a day exploring Central Park, visiting the Metropolitan Museum of Art, and then strolling down Fifth Avenue without ever needing to take a cab or subway. In neighbourhoods like Greenwich Village, SoHo, and the Lower East Side, walking is the best way to soak in the local atmosphere and discover unique shops, restaurants, and historic sites.

Another benefit of walking in New York is the opportunity to interact with the city's diverse communities. Each neighbourhood has its own character and rhythm, shaped by the people who live and work there. Walking through the different areas of the city, you'll experience a tapestry of cultures, languages, and traditions. This diversity is reflected in the food, the architecture, and the street life, offering a rich and varied experience at every turn.

Walking is also a great way to avoid the traffic and delays that can come with other forms of transportation. New York's streets can be busy, especially during rush hour, but as a pedestrian, you have the advantage of being able to move at your own pace, navigate around congested areas, and take shortcuts through parks or quieter side streets. This makes walking a particularly appealing option during peak travel times when other transportation options might be slower or less reliable.

Safety is an important consideration when walking in any city, and New York is no exception. While the city is generally safe for pedestrians, it's important to stay aware of your surroundings, especially when crossing streets. New York drivers can be aggressive, and it's crucial to use crosswalks and obey traffic signals. Many of the city's busiest streets have pedestrian crossings that are well-marked and timed to allow safe passage across major avenues. In some areas, pedestrian plazas have been created to provide a space where people can walk, sit, and relax without the need to navigate traffic.

The physical benefits of walking are also significant. With so much to see and do, walking in New York is not just about getting from point A to point B—it's an enjoyable way to stay active. Walking through the city's many parks, along the waterfront, or through bustling neighbourhoods provides a good workout while also engaging the mind with the sights and sounds of urban life. Whether you're on a leisurely stroll or a brisk walk, exploring New York on foot keeps you moving and energised.

Walking also offers a sense of spontaneity that is often lacking in more structured forms of transportation. When you walk, you have the freedom to change your plans on a whim—to take a different route, explore a new neighbourhood, or simply follow your curiosity. This sense of adventure is one of the most rewarding aspects of walking in New York, where even the most ordinary street can lead to an extraordinary discovery.

For visitors to the city, walking is often the best way to get adjusted. The pace of walking allows you to take in your surroundings, orient yourself, and become familiar with the layout of the city. It also gives you the chance to observe the daily life of New Yorkers, from the early morning rush to the late-night energy of the city that never sleeps. This immersion into the rhythm of the city helps you feel connected and more at ease, making your visit more enjoyable.

Lastly, walking in New York is an environmentally friendly way to travel. With no emissions and no fuel required, walking contributes to a cleaner, greener city. As more people choose to walk, the city becomes more pedestrian-friendly, with increased investment in sidewalks, pedestrian plazas, and other infrastructure that supports a walkable environment. By choosing to explore the city on foot, you're not only enjoying a healthier and more engaging experience, but you're also helping to reduce your carbon footprint and contribute to a more sustainable urban environment.

Walking is one of the most fulfilling ways to experience New York City. It allows you to connect with the city on a personal level, explore its many neighbourhoods and attractions at your own pace, and enjoy the physical and environmental benefits of moving on foot. Whether you're a first-time visitor or a seasoned New Yorker, walking through the city offers endless opportunities for discovery, making it an essential part of any New York City experience.

Driving

Driving in New York presents a unique set of challenges and rewards. The city's streets are a constant flurry of activity, filled with pedestrians, cyclists, taxis, buses, and other vehicles. For those who choose to drive, whether out of necessity or preference, understanding the nuances of navigating these busy streets is crucial. Driving in New York can be daunting for the uninitiated, but with the right knowledge and preparation, it can also offer a level of convenience and flexibility that other modes of transportation may not provide.

One of the primary reasons travellers might consider driving in New York City is the freedom it offers to explore beyond the reach of public transportation. While the subway and buses cover much of the city, there are certain areas—particularly in the outer boroughs or along the edges of the city—where driving is the most efficient way to get around. Additionally, for those travelling with a group or carrying a significant amount of luggage, having a car can make transportation much easier and more comfortable.

Navigating New York City's streets requires a good understanding of the city's layout and traffic patterns. Manhattan is organised in a grid system, with numbered streets running east to west and avenues running north to south. This grid system makes it relatively easy to understand directions and estimate travel times. However, the sheer density of the city means that even short trips can take longer than expected due to traffic congestion, particularly during peak hours. Familiarising yourself with the main thoroughfares, one-way streets, and alternative routes can help you navigate the city more effectively.

Traffic in New York City is in constant presence, and it is important to be prepared for delays. Rush hour in the morning and evening can significantly increase travel times, especially in busy areas like Midtown Manhattan or near bridges and tunnels. Parking can also be a significant challenge. Street parking is limited, and parking regulations are strictly enforced, with frequent street cleaning schedules, meters, and restricted areas. Many drivers opt to use paid parking garages, which are available throughout the city but can be expensive, especially in central locations.

Driving in New York City also means sharing the road with a wide variety of other users, from aggressive taxi drivers to unpredictable pedestrians and cyclists. Defensive driving is essential, as is a good understanding of the city's traffic rules and signals. New York is known for its heavy use of horns, and drivers need to be assertive while remaining patient. Pedestrians often cross the street outside of crosswalks or against the light, so staying alert is crucial to avoid accidents. It's also important to note that certain areas of the city, like Times Square, are pedestrian zones where vehicles are restricted or prohibited entirely.

For those unfamiliar with the city, using a GPS or navigation app is highly recommended. These tools can help you avoid traffic jams, find the best routes, and locate parking. Many apps also provide real-time updates on traffic conditions, road closures, and other potential delays, allowing you to adjust your route as needed. However, it's important to keep in mind that New York's tall buildings can sometimes interfere with GPS signals, so having a basic understanding of your route beforehand is always a good idea.

Another aspect of driving in New York City to consider is the toll system. Many of the bridges and tunnels leading into Manhattan charge tolls, which can add up over the course of a trip. Tolls are often collected electronically through systems like E-ZPass, which automatically deducts the toll from a prepaid account. For those without E-ZPass, tolls can be paid by mail, but this often incurs an additional fee. Planning your route to avoid tolls, when possible, can help reduce costs, although this may increase travel time.

In addition to the regular traffic challenges, drivers in New York City must also be prepared for the occasional street closures due to events, parades, or construction. These closures can disrupt normal traffic patterns and cause significant detours, especially in busy areas. Checking local news or traffic updates before heading out can help you avoid unexpected delays and find alternate routes if necessary.

Despite the challenges, there are several benefits to driving in New York City. One of the most significant is the ability to explore areas that are less accessible by public transportation. Neighbourhoods in the outer boroughs, such as Staten Island, parts of Queens, and the Bronx, are more easily reached by car, and having a vehicle can make visiting these areas more convenient. Additionally, driving allows for more flexibility in terms of schedule and route, giving you the freedom to change your plans on the go.

Driving also offers a unique perspective on the city. While walking and public transportation immerse you in the energy and pace of New York, driving provides a broader view, allowing you to see the city's skyline, bridges, and landmarks from different angles. This can be particularly rewarding during off-peak hours when traffic is lighter and the city takes on a different, more relaxed character.

For visitors who prefer not to navigate the city's streets themselves, hiring a private driver or using car services can provide many of the benefits of driving without the stress. Private car services offer professional drivers who are familiar with the city's traffic patterns and can handle parking, tolls, and route planning. This option is particularly useful for business travellers, special occasions, or those who want to travel in comfort and style.

While driving in New York City presents its own set of challenges, it also offers a level of convenience and flexibility that can enhance your experience of the city. By understanding the city's layout, traffic patterns, and parking regulations, and by staying alert and prepared, driving can be a viable and even enjoyable way to navigate the many wonders that New York has to offer.

Accessibility Tips for Travellers with Mobility Issues

Navigating New York City can be challenging for anyone, but it presents specific considerations for travellers with mobility issues. However, with some planning and the right information, the city can be accessible and enjoyable. New York City has made significant strides in recent years to accommodate travellers with disabilities, offering various services, infrastructure improvements, and accessible transportation options that cater to those with mobility challenges.

One of the most important aspects of planning a trip to New York for travellers with mobility issues is understanding the transportation options that are available. The city's public transportation system, including the subway, buses, and taxis, has several features designed to assist those who require accessible services. Although the subway system is extensive, not all stations are fully accessible. Many stations have elevators and ramps, but it's essential to plan your route carefully to ensure that the stations you intend to use are equipped with these facilities. The MTA website and various transit apps provide detailed information on which stations are accessible, allowing travellers to map out their journeys in advance.

Buses in New York City are generally more accessible than the subway. All city buses are equipped with ramps or lifts and designated areas for wheelchairs and other mobility devices. The bus system can be a more straightforward option for those who need to avoid stairs, as it provides access to areas that may not be serviced by accessible subway stations. Buses also offer the advantage of stopping frequently, making it easier to reach destinations that might be a longer walk from the nearest subway station.

Taxis and rideshares are another option for travellers with mobility issues. New York City has a large fleet of accessible taxis, which are equipped with ramps and are spacious enough to accommodate wheelchairs. These taxis can be hailed from the street or booked in advance through accessible dispatch services. Rideshare companies also offer vehicles with accessibility features, and passengers can request a wheelchair-accessible vehicle (WAV) directly from their apps. These services provide a convenient and flexible way to travel around the city, especially for those who prefer not to navigate public transportation.

Sidewalks and pedestrian areas in New York City have also been improved to enhance accessibility. Curb cuts at intersections allow for smoother transitions between the street and the sidewalk, making it easier for those using wheelchairs, scooters, or other mobility devices to move around the city. Additionally, many public spaces, parks, and attractions have been designed or modified to be accessible. For example, Central Park has several accessible pathways and entrances, and many of the city's museums and theatres offer accessible seating and services.

When visiting tourist attractions, it's helpful to know in advance which sites offer accessible features. Most of New York's major attractions, such as the Statue of Liberty, the Empire State Building, and the Metropolitan Museum of

Art, are equipped with elevators, ramps, and accessible restrooms. Many attractions also offer additional services, such as guided tours tailored to visitors with mobility issues or special accommodations for those with specific needs. Checking the accessibility information on the websites of these attractions or contacting them directly before your visit can help ensure a smooth experience.

Hotels in New York City offer a range of accessibility features, but it's important to confirm these when making a reservation. Accessible rooms typically include features such as wider doorways, roll-in showers, grab bars, and lower beds and counters. Some hotels also provide additional services, such as assistance with transportation or arrangements for medical equipment rentals. When booking, be sure to communicate your specific needs to ensure that your accommodation meets your requirements.

For those who may need assistance navigating the city, several organisations and services are available to help. These can range from personal care attendants to mobility equipment rentals, which can be arranged before your arrival. Many of these services can be coordinated through your hotel or through specialised travel agencies that focus on accessibility.

Navigating the city's busy streets can be challenging, even for able-bodied travellers, so it's advisable to allow extra time to reach your destination. Patience and a flexible schedule can help reduce the stress of getting around. Having a companion or using a guide service can also make the experience more manageable, particularly if you are visiting for the first time.

It's also essential to stay informed about the weather, as New York's sidewalks and streets can become slippery in the rain or snow. Proper footwear and protective gear for your mobility device can help ensure a safer journey. If the weather is particularly harsh, taxis and rideshares offer a good alternative to walking or using public transportation.

Finally, New York City is home to several advocacy groups and resources dedicated to improving accessibility and providing support to those with disabilities. These organisations can offer valuable advice, resources, and support before and during your trip. Reaching out to these groups can provide peace of mind and ensure that you have all the necessary information to make your visit as comfortable as possible.

While travelling in New York City with mobility issues requires careful planning, the city offers many resources and services to ensure that all travellers can enjoy its many attractions and experiences. By taking advantage of accessible transportation options, staying informed about accessible routes and attractions, and using the available resources, travellers with mobility challenges can navigate the city with confidence and make the most of their time in this xciting destination.

Understanding how to navigate New York City is essential to fully enjoying everything it has to offer. With a little preparation and the right approach, getting to and around the city can be both efficient and stress-free. By familiarising yourself with the available transportation options, you'll be well-equipped to explore the city with confidence and ease, making your time in New York truly memorable.

CHAPTER 4

Accomodation

Finding the right place to stay is an important part of planning your visit to New York City. The city offers a wide range of accommodation options, each providing its own unique experience. With so many choices, it's possible to find a place that suits your preferences and needs.

Luxury Hotels and Resorts

The Plaza Hotel

The Plaza Hotel, often referred to simply as "The Plaza," is an iconic landmark in New York City. Located on the edge of Central Park, this hotel is known for its opulent décor, luxurious amenities, and impeccable service. A stay at The Plaza offers a quintessential New York experience, combining elegance with modern conveniences. Room rates typically start at around $1,000 per night but can vary significantly depending on the season and room type.

Scan the Qr code to book The Plaza Hotel

From JFK Airport, you can reach The Plaza by taxi in about 40 minutes, depending on traffic, or by taking the AirTrain to Jamaica Station, followed by the E subway to Fifth Avenue/53rd Street. From LaGuardia, a taxi or rideshare will take about 30 minutes. Newark Airport is about a 45-minute drive, or you can take the AirTrain to Newark Liberty Station, then a New Jersey Transit train to Penn Station, followed by a short taxi ride, or the E subway to Fifth Avenue/53rd Street.

Transportation Options

The Plaza is centrally located with easy access to the NYC subway, buses, and taxis. Valet parking is available for guests, and the hotel also offers limousine services.

Navigation and Directions

The hotel sits at the corner of Fifth Avenue and Central Park South, making it easily accessible from Midtown Manhattan. The N, Q, and R subway lines stop nearby at Fifth Avenue/59th Street, and several bus routes serve the area.

Recommended Restaurants

The Plaza offers exquisite dining options such as The Palm Court, known for its afternoon tea, and The Rose Club for cocktails. Nearby, you'll find celebrated restaurants like Per Se at the Time Warner Centre and Nobu 57.

Nearby Attractions

Central Park is right at your doorstep, offering scenic walks and the Central Park Zoo. The Museum of Modern Art (MoMA) and Rockefeller Centre are also just a short stroll away.

The Ritz-Carlton New York, Central Park

The Ritz-Carlton New York, Central Park, is synonymous with luxury and refinement. Overlooking Central Park, this five-star hotel portrays classic elegance and contemporary style. Guests enjoy personalised service and high-end amenities, including a renowned spa. Room rates start at approximately $1,200 per night.

Scan the Qr code to book The Ritz-Carlton New York, Central Park

From JFK, you can take a taxi or the AirTrain to Jamaica Station, then transfer to the E subway line to 57th Street. From LaGuardia, a taxi or rideshare takes around 30 minutes. Newark Airport is about 45 minutes away by taxi, or you can take a combination of AirTrain, NJ Transit, and subway.

Transportation Options

This hotel is well-connected by subway, with the N, Q, and R lines stopping nearby at 57th Street. Taxis and rideshares are readily available, and the hotel provides valet parking and limousine services.

Navigation and Directions

Located at 50 Central Park South, the hotel is accessible from several key subway lines, including the A, C, B, D, and 1 trains at Columbus Circle.

Recommended Restaurants

The hotel's Auden Bistro & Bar offers an upscale dining experience with views of Central Park. Nearby dining options include Jean-Georges at the Trump International Hotel and The Modern at MoMA.

Nearby Attractions

Guests can explore Central Park, visit the American Museum of Natural History, or shop along Fifth Avenue. The Broadway theatres are also within walking distance.

The St. Regis New York

The St. Regis New York, located on Fifth Avenue, is a hallmark of luxury and sophistication. Known for its bespoke butler service and timeless design, this hotel is a favourite among those seeking an opulent stay in the heart of the city. Room rates generally start at around $1,100 per night.

Scan the Qr code to book The St. Regis New York

From JFK, you can reach The St. Regis by taxi in about 40 minutes or take the AirTrain to Jamaica Station, followed by the E subway to 53rd Street. LaGuardia is about a 30-minute taxi ride away, while Newark is about 45 minutes by taxi, or you can take a combination of AirTrain, NJ Transit, and subway.

Transportation Options

The hotel is conveniently located near the 5th Avenue/53rd Street subway station (E and M lines) and 59th Street (N, Q, R lines). Taxis, rideshares, and the hotel's chauffeur service are available.

Navigation and Directions

Positioned at the corner of Fifth Avenue and 55th Street, The St. Regis is easily accessible by subway, taxi, or on foot from other Midtown attractions. The hotel's central location makes navigating the city straightforward.

Recommended Restaurants

Inside the hotel, Astor Court provides a fine dining experience with American cuisine. Nearby, try the Michelin-starred Le Bernardin for exceptional seafood or Avra Estiatorio for upscale Greek cuisine.

Nearby Attractions

Just a short walk from The St. Regis are some of New York's most famous landmarks, including the Rockefeller Centre, St. Patrick's Cathedral, and the shops of Fifth Avenue. MoMA and Central Park are also nearby.

Mid-Range Hotels and Boutique Options

Library Hotel

The Library Hotel is a unique boutique hotel that offers a literary-themed experience. Each of its ten floors is dedicated to a different category of the Dewey Decimal System, with rooms filled with books related to the theme. Located near Bryant Park and the New York Public Library, it's perfect for book lovers. Room rates typically start around $350 per night.

Scan the Qr code to book Library Hotel

From JFK, you can take a taxi, which takes about 45 minutes, or the AirTrain to Jamaica Station, then the E subway line to 42nd Street-Bryant Park. From LaGuardia, a taxi will take about 30 minutes. Newark Airport is about 45 minutes by taxi or a combination of AirTrain and NJ Transit to Penn Station, followed by a short subway ride or taxi.

Transportation Options

The hotel is close to several subway lines, including the B, D, F, and M lines at Bryant Park. Taxis and rideshares are also readily available.

Navigation and Directions

Located on Madison Avenue between 41st and 42nd Streets, the hotel is easily accessible by subway, bus, or on foot from many Midtown attractions.

Recommended Restaurants

The hotel's rooftop, Bookmarks Lounge, offers cocktails and light bites. Nearby, you can dine at upscale options like Ai Fiori in the Langham Hotel or grab a quick meal at the Bryant Park Grill.

Nearby Attractions

The New York Public Library, Bryant Park, and Grand Central Terminal are just steps away, while Times Square and the Empire State Building are within a short walk.

The Greenwich Hotel

Located in Tribeca, The Greenwich Hotel offers an intimate, luxury experience with a strong emphasis on design and comfort. The rooms are uniquely decorated with a blend of global influences. Rates start around $900 per night.

Scan the Qr code to book The Greenwich Hotel

From JFK, the best option is a taxi, taking around 45 minutes. Alternatively, use the AirTrain and A subway line to Canal Street. From LaGuardia, a taxi will take about 30 minutes, while Newark Airport is about 45 minutes by taxi or NJ Transit.

Transportation Options

The hotel is close to the 1, A, C, and E subway lines, offering easy access to the rest of Manhattan. Taxis and rideshares are also plentiful in Tribeca.

Navigation and Directions

Situated at 377 Greenwich Street, The Greenwich Hotel is well-connected by public transport and is an easy walk to many downtown attractions.

Recommended Restaurants

Onsite, the hotel's restaurant, Locanda Verde, serves Italian cuisine in a cosy setting. Nearby, you'll find Nobu and the Odeon, both renowned dining spots.

Nearby Attractions

Visit the nearby 9/11 Memorial & Museum, take a walk along the Hudson River Park, or explore the trendy shops and galleries in Tribeca.

The Marlton Hotel

The Marlton Hotel, located in Greenwich Village, offers a stylish yet affordable option in a historic building. The rooms are small but thoughtfully designed, making it a great choice for solo travellers or couples. Room rates start around $300 per night.

Scan the Qr code to book The Marlton Hotel

From JFK, take a taxi (45 minutes) or use the AirTrain and subway (E train to West 4th Street-Washington Square). From LaGuardia, a taxi takes about 30 minutes. Newark is about 45 minutes by taxi, or you can take NJ Transit to Penn Station and transfer to the subway.

Transportation Options

The hotel is close to the A, B, C, D, E, F, and M subway lines, providing easy access to the rest of Manhattan. Taxis and rideshares are readily available.

Navigation and Directions

Located at 5 West 8th Street, The Marlton is in the heart of Greenwich Village, easily reachable by subway or taxi. It's an ideal location for exploring downtown Manhattan.

Recommended Restaurants

The hotel's restaurant, Margaux, offers a farm-to-table dining experience. Nearby, you can enjoy meals at Carbone, an Italian-American restaurant, or Blue Hill, a farm-to-table dining spot.

Nearby Attractions

Explore Washington Square Park, visit NYU's campus, or stroll through the vibrant streets of Greenwich Village. The Whitney Museum of American Art and the High Line are also nearby.

Budget Stays

HI New York City Hostel

HI The New York City Hostel, part of the Hostelling International chain, is one of the largest and most popular hostels in NYC. It's located on the Upper West Side, offering a communal and budget-friendly experience with dormitory-style rooms starting at around $50 per night. The hostel features shared kitchens, free Wi-Fi, and a spacious outdoor patio, making it ideal for travellers looking to meet new people while exploring the city.

From JFK, take the AirTrain to Howard Beach, then the A train to 59th Street-Columbus Circle, and transfer to the 1 train to 103rd Street. From LaGuardia, take the M60 SBS bus to Broadway and 106th Street. From Newark, use NJ Transit to Penn Station, then the 1 train uptown to 103rd Street.

Transportation Options

The hostel is conveniently located near the 103rd Street subway station on the 1 line, offering easy access to the rest of the city. Buses and rideshares are also available, and cycling enthusiasts can take advantage of nearby bike rental stations.

Navigation and Directions

Located at 891 Amsterdam Avenue, the hostel is easy to reach by subway or bus. From 103rd Street, it's just a short walk north to the hostel.

Booking Information

Book directly through the HI Hostels website or through popular booking sites like Hostelworld and Booking.com. Early booking is recommended, especially during peak travel seasons.

Recommended Restaurants

Nearby, you'll find great dining options like Absolute Bagels for breakfast and The Tang for modern Chinese cuisine. For a cosy dinner, try Carmine's for Italian-American fare.

Nearby Attractions

Riverside Park is just a few blocks away, offering scenic views of the Hudson River. Central Park, the American Museum of Natural History, and Columbia University are all within walking distance.

The Jane Hotel

The Jane Hotel in the West Village offers a quirky yet charming stay in the heart of New York. Originally built as a sailor's hotel in 1908, it features compact, cabin-like rooms with vintage décor. Prices start at around $200 per night, making it an affordable option with a touch of historic charm.

Scan the Qr code to book The Jane Hotel

From JFK, take the AirTrain to Howard Beach, then the A train to 14th Street, followed by a short walk to the hotel. From LaGuardia, take the M60 SBS to 125th Street, then the 1 train to 14th Street. From Newark, take NJ Transit to Penn Station, then the A, C, or E train to 14th Street.

Transportation Options

The hotel is close to the 14th Street subway station (A, C, E, L lines), offering easy access to all of Manhattan. Buses and taxis are also readily available.

Navigation and Directions

The Jane Hotel is located at 113 Jane Street, in the trendy Meatpacking District. From the 14th Street station, it's a short walk west towards the Hudson River.

Recommended Restaurants

The hotel's Café Gitane offers French-Moroccan cuisine in a stylish setting. Nearby, you'll find The Standard Grill and Chelsea Market, both offering a variety of dining options.

Nearby Attractions

The High Line, an elevated park built on a former rail line, is just a block away. The Whitney Museum of American Art and the vibrant nightlife of the Meatpacking District are also within walking distance.

Pod 39 Hotel

Pod 39 Hotel in Midtown Manhattan is a modern, budget-friendly option known for its efficient use of space and vibrant social atmosphere. Rooms are compact but comfortable, with rates starting at around $200 per night. The hotel features a rooftop bar with panoramic views and a playful, colourful design throughout.

Scan the Qr code to book Pod 39 Hotel

From JFK, take the airtrain to Jamaica Station, then the E train to Lexington Avenue/53rd Street, followed by a short walk. From LaGuardia, the Q70 SBS bus to Jackson Heights-Roosevelt Avenue, then the E train to Lexington Avenue. Newark travellers can take NJ Transit to Penn Station, then transfer to the 6 train to 33rd Street.

Transportation Options

Pod 39 is near the 33rd Street subway station on the 6 line, providing quick access to the rest of the city. Grand Central Terminal is also nearby, offering connections to multiple subway lines.

Navigation and Directions

Located at 145 East 39th Street, the hotel is easily accessible by subway, bus, or on foot from many Midtown attractions.

Recommended Restaurants

Onsite, Salvation Taco offers a unique blend of Mexican and global flavors. Nearby, visit Sarge's Delicatessen for classic New York deli fare or The Capital Grille for upscale dining.

Nearby Attractions

Grand Central Terminal, the Chrysler Building, and the New York Public Library are all within a short walk. The Empire State Building and Times Square are also easily accessible.

Freehand New York

Freehand New York in the Flatiron District offers an artsy and affordable stay with a creative atmosphere. Housed in a historic building, the hotel features eclectic décor and a variety of room types, including shared accommodations. Prices start at around $200 per night.

From JFK, take the AirTrain to Jamaica Station, then the E train to 23rd Street. From LaGuardia, take the Q70 SBS bus to Jackson Heights, then the E train to 23rd Street. Newark travellers can take NJ Transit to Penn Station, followed by the 1 train to 23rd Street.

Transportation Options

The hotel is near the 23rd Street subway station (R and W lines), offering easy access to downtown and uptown Manhattan. Buses and rideshares are also available.

Navigation and Directions

Located at 23 Lexington Avenue, Freehand New York is easily accessible by subway, with the 23rd Street station just a few steps away.

Booking Information

Book directly on the Freehand website for exclusive offers or use popular booking platforms like Expedia or Hotels.com.

Recommended Restaurants

The hotel's restaurant, Simon & The Whale, offers a trendy dining experience with a seasonal menu. Nearby, try Gramercy Tavern for a New American menu or The Smith for a classic NYC brasserie experience.

Nearby Attractions

Madison Square Park, the Flatiron Building, and Union Square are all within walking distance. The Museum of Sex and the Rubin Museum of Art are also nearby, offering unique cultural experiences.

Vacation Rentals and Short Term Apartments

AKA Central Park

AKA Central Park offers luxury extended-stay apartments with the comfort of home and the amenities of a high-end hotel. Located just steps from Central Park, these modern, fully furnished apartments range from studios to penthouses, with prices starting around $300 per night for short-term stays. With a focus on privacy and comfort, AKA is perfect for both business travellers and vacationers.

From JFK, you can take a taxi, which takes about 45 minutes, or the AirTrain to Jamaica Station, followed by the E subway line to 53rd Street, then a quick walk to the hotel. From LaGuardia, a taxi will take around 30 minutes, or you can take the Q70 SBS bus to Jackson Heights-Roosevelt Avenue, then transfer to the F train to 57th Street. Newark Airport is about 45 minutes away by taxi, or you can take NJ Transit to Penn Station, followed by the A, C, or E train to 59th Street-Columbus Circle.

Transportation Options

The property is well-connected by subway, with the 57th Street and 59th Street-Columbus Circle stations nearby, providing access to the N, Q, R, W, A, B, C, and D lines. Taxis, buses, and rideshares are also readily available.

Navigation and Directions

Located at 42 West 58th Street, AKA Central Park is easily accessible by public transportation or a short taxi ride from most Midtown destinations. The location is ideal for exploring Central Park, Fifth Avenue, and the surrounding areas.

Booking Information

Bookings can be made directly on the AKA website or through platforms like Booking.com and Expedia. Special offers may be available for longer stays.

Recommended Restaurants

Nearby dining options include the upscale Jean-Georges for a gourmet meal or P.J. Clarke's for a classic American dining experience. The Plaza Food Hall, located nearby, offers a variety of dining options in a casual setting.

Nearby Attractions

Central Park is just steps away, offering everything from scenic walks to boat rides. The Museum of Modern Art (MoMA) and Rockefeller Centre are also within walking distance.

The Beekman Tower

The Beekman Tower offers stylish, fully furnished apartments in a historic building in Midtown East. With studios, one- and two-bedroom apartments available, it's perfect for both short and extended stays. Prices start around $250 per night for short-term stays. The apartments combine modern amenities with classic New York charm, providing a comfortable home base for exploring the city.

From JFK, take the AirTrain to Jamaica Station, then the E subway line to Lexington Avenue/53rd Street. From LaGuardia, a taxi takes about 30 minutes, or you can take the Q70 SBS bus to Jackson Heights-Roosevelt Avenue and then the E train. Newark Airport is about 45 minutes away by taxi, or you can take NJ Transit to Penn Station, then the E train to Lexington Avenue.

Transportation Options

The Beekman Tower is conveniently located near the 51st Street subway station, providing easy access to the 6 line. Several bus routes also serve the area, and taxis are readily available.

Navigation and Directions

Situated at 3 Mitchell Place, The Beekman Tower is easily accessible by subway, bus, or taxi. Its central location makes it easy to reach many of Midtown's attractions.

Booking Information

Reservations can be made directly on The Beekman Tower's website or through major booking platforms like Hotels.com and Agoda.

Recommended Restaurants

Tudor City Steakhouse, just a short walk away, offers classic steakhouse fare in an elegant setting. For a casual meal, head to Ess-a-Bagel for some of the city's best bagels.

Nearby Attractions

The United Nations Headquarters is nearby, offering tours and exhibitions. Also close are Grand Central Terminal and the Chrysler Building, both iconic New York landmarks.

The Standard, East Village

The Standard, East Village, offers chic, modern apartments in one of New York's most vibrant neighborhoods. Known for its artistic flair and hip vibe, the hotel provides both short-term and extended-stay options, with prices starting around $350 per night. The apartments are stylishly furnished and offer stunning views of the city skyline.

Scan the Qr code to book The Standard, East Village

From JFK, take the AirTrain to Jamaica Station, then the E subway to 14th Street, transferring to the L line to First Avenue. From LaGuardia, a taxi takes about 25 minutes, or take the Q70 SBS to Jackson Heights and transfer to the E and L lines. Newark Airport is about 40 minutes away by taxi, or you can take NJ Transit to Penn Station and then transfer to the subway.

Transportation Options

The hotel is close to the Astor Place and 8th Street subway stations, providing access to the 4, 6, N, and R lines. The area is also well served by buses and taxis.

Navigation and Directions

Located at 25 Cooper Square, The Standard, East Village is easy to reach by public transportation or taxi. The neighbourhood is known for its bohemian atmosphere and is a great base for exploring downtown Manhattan.

Recommended Restaurants

The Standard's on-site restaurant, Narcissa, offers farm-to-table cuisine in a stylish setting. Nearby, you'll find the iconic Veselka, a 24-hour Ukrainian diner, and Momofuku Noodle Bar for inventive ramen dishes.

Nearby Attractions

Washington Square Park, the New Museum, and the vibrant streets of the East Village are all within walking distance. The area is also home to numerous theatres, galleries, and music venues.

The Smyth Tribeca

The Smyth Tribeca offers luxury apartments in the trendy Tribeca neighborhood. These fully furnished apartments are available for both short-term and extended stays, with prices starting around $350 per night. The apartments feature contemporary design, high-end finishes, and a host of amenities, making them the perfect choice for a comfortable and stylish stay in New York City.

From JFK, take the AirTrain to Howard Beach, then the A train to Canal Street. From LaGuardia, take the Q70 SBS to

Jackson Heights, then the E train to Canal Street. Newark travellers can take NJ Transit to Penn Station, then transfer to the 1 train to Franklin Street.

Transportation Options

The Smyth Tribeca is near the Franklin Street subway station, offering access to the 1 train. Other nearby stations provide access to the A, C, E, and R lines. Taxis, buses, and rideshares are also easily accessible.

Navigation and Directions

Located at 85 West Broadway, The Smyth Tribeca is conveniently positioned for exploring downtown Manhattan. The hotel is just a short walk from the subway, and its central location makes it easy to navigate the city.

Booking Information

Bookings can be made directly through The Smyth's website or through platforms like Booking.com and Hotels.com.

Recommended Restaurants

The Smyth's restaurant, Little Park, offers seasonal, farm-to-table dining in a sophisticated setting. Nearby, visit The Odeon for classic French-American fare or Locanda Verde for upscale Italian dining.

Nearby Attractions

The 9/11 Memorial & Museum, One World Observatory, and the Hudson River Park are all within easy reach. Tribeca's cobblestone streets are also home to art galleries, boutiques, and trendy cafes.

Tips for Finding Last-Minute Deals

Use Specialised Apps and Websites

Platforms like HotelTonight, Expedia, and Booking.com often offer significant discounts on unsold rooms. These apps are designed specifically for last-minute travellers and can help you secure deals at a fraction of the usual cost.

Check for Direct Booking Offers

Many hotels provide last-minute deals directly on their websites or through their customer service lines. Always check the hotel's official site before booking elsewhere.

Be Flexible with Dates

If your travel dates are flexible, use this to your advantage. Mid-week stays, especially on Tuesday or Wednesday, often have lower rates than weekends.

Consider Different Neighborhoods

Exploring beyond Midtown or Times Square can lead to cheaper accommodations. Areas like Brooklyn, Long Island City, or Harlem can offer excellent deals while still being a short subway ride away from the main attractions.

Sign Up for Alerts

Many booking platforms and hotels offer email alerts for last-minute deals. Signing up for these can keep you informed of price drops and exclusive offers.

Utilise Loyalty Programs

If you're a member of any hotel loyalty programs, you might find special last-minute rates or point discounts that aren't available to the general public.

Call the Hotel Directly

Sometimes, calling the hotel directly and enquiring about last-minute availability can result in better rates than those listed online, especially if they have unsold rooms.

Consider Vacation Rentals

Sites like Airbnb or Vrbo might have hosts willing to drop their prices to fill up last-minute availability. Look for "instant booking" options that allow you to secure a place immediately.

Avoid High-Traffic Seasons

Travelling outside peak tourist seasons can improve your chances of finding a last-minute deal. Times like early January or late summer often have better availability at lower prices.

Check for Package Deals

Sometimes booking a flight and hotel together can lead to significant savings, even if you're booking last minute. Websites like Expedia and Travelocity offer package deals that can be cheaper than booking separately.

Choosing where to stay in New York City is an important part of making your visit memorable. With so many options, there's something to suit every kind of traveller. The key is to find a place that fits your needs and allows you to experience the city comfortably. Wherever you decide to stay, you'll be well-positioned to explore everything that New York has to offer, ensuring a trip filled with excitement and discovery.

CHAPTER 5

Top Attractions

New York City is a place that constantly surprises and excites visitors with its endless array of attractions. Each corner of the city offers something unique waiting to be explored. Get ready to discover the places that make this city one of the most fascinating destinations in the world, offering something new and unforgettable at every turn.

Iconic Landmarks

New York City is home to some of the most recognisable landmarks in the world. These iconic places are must-see attractions for any visitor. Here's a closer look at some of these landmarks.

Statue of Liberty

The Statue of Liberty stands as a symbol of freedom and democracy, gifted by France to the United States in 1886. It is located on Liberty Island in New York Harbour and has welcomed millions of immigrants arriving by sea. The statue is not only a national monument but also a UNESCO World Heritage site, representing hope and opportunity.

To visit, you'll need to take a ferry from Battery Park in Manhattan or Liberty State Park in New Jersey. Ferries operate daily, generally from 8:30 AM to 4:00 PM, though hours can vary depending on the season. Visitors are encouraged to arrive early to avoid long lines. Once on the island, you can explore the grounds, visit the museum, and, if you've reserved a ticket in advance, climb up to the crown for a stunning view of the harbour.

The experience is budget-friendly, with ferry tickets costing around $25 for adults. However, crown access requires an additional fee and must be booked months in advance due to limited availability. Visitors should be prepared for airport-style security checks before boarding the ferry and are advised to wear comfortable shoes for walking and climbing.

Scan the Qr code to book The Statue of Liberty

The Statue of Liberty represents more than just a tourist attraction; it embodies the spirit of New York and the ideals of the nation. As you walk around the island, you'll find various plaques and exhibits detailing the history and significance of the statue, enhancing your understanding of this remarkable monument.

Empire State Building

The Empire State Building is one of New York City's most famous skyscrapers, soaring 1,454 feet into the sky. Completed in 1931, it held the title of the world's tallest building for nearly 40 years and remains an architectural marvel. Located at 350 Fifth Avenue in Midtown Manhattan, it is a prime example of Art Deco design and a symbol of American ambition and innovation.

The building is open to visitors from 9:00 AM to midnight, with the last elevator ride to the observation decks at 11:15 PM. The main observation deck on the 86th floor offers breathtaking views of the city, while the 102nd-floor deck provides an even more elevated perspective. Tickets start at around $45 for the standard admission, with higher prices for VIP experiences or access to the 102nd floor.

Reaching the Empire State Building is easy, thanks to its central location. The building is accessible via multiple subway lines, including the B, D, F, M, N, Q, R, and W trains, all of which stop nearby. Taxis and buses are also readily available.

Scan the Qr code to book The Empire State Building

As you explore, you'll find a variety of exhibits detailing the building's construction, its role in popular culture, and its place in New York's history. The Empire State Building has been featured in countless films and TV shows, cementing its status as an icon. Expect to spend about an hour or two touring the observation decks and exhibits, taking in the panoramic views, and learning about the history of this legendary skyscraper.

The iconic landmarks offer a glimpse into the heart and history of New York City. Each of these sites provides an unforgettable experience that captures the spirit of the city.

Historic Landmarks and Monuments

New York City is rich with history and historic landmarks. Here are some of the landmarks.

The Brooklyn Bridge

The Brooklyn Bridge is one of the oldest suspension bridges in the United States, connecting the boroughs of Manhattan and Brooklyn over the East River. Completed in 1883, it was an engineering marvel of its time and remains an iconic symbol of New York City. The bridge is renowned for its Gothic-style arches and steel cables, making it a favourite spot for both locals and tourists.

Located between Manhattan and Brooklyn, you can start your journey on either side. From Manhattan, the entrance is near City Hall Park, while in Brooklyn, the entrance is at the intersection of Tillary Street and Adams Street. The bridge is easily accessible via multiple subway lines; in Manhattan, the 4, 5, and 6 trains stop at Brooklyn Bridge-City Hall, and in Brooklyn, the A, C, or F trains stop at High Street-Brooklyn Bridge.

The bridge is open 24/7, and there is no cost to walk or bike across it. It's a pedestrian-friendly route with a dedicated walkway, separate from the vehicular lanes. As you walk across, you'll enjoy breathtaking views of the Manhattan skyline, the Statue of Liberty, and the surrounding waterways. It's a popular spot for photography, so expect to see many others taking in the sights.

Crossing the bridge can take anywhere from 20 to 40 minutes, depending on your pace and how often you stop to take photos. The best times to visit are early in the morning or late in the evening when the bridge is less crowded. Along the way, you'll encounter plaques and markers that detail the history and construction of the bridge, providing a deeper understanding of its significance.

Ellis Island National Museum of Immigration

Ellis Island was the primary immigration station in the United States from 1892 to 1954, where over 12 million immigrants passed through on their way to becoming American citizens. Today, it houses the Ellis Island National Museum of Immigration, which preserves the history and personal stories of those who came through its halls. The museum offers a poignant look at the immigrant experience and the diverse roots of the American population.

To visit Ellis Island, you'll need to take the same ferry that serves the Statue of Liberty, departing from Battery Park in Manhattan or Liberty State Park in New Jersey. The ferry operates daily from 9:00 AM to 4:30 PM, with extended hours during peak seasons. A ticket costs around $25 for adults, which includes access to both the Statue of Liberty and Ellis Island.

Upon arrival, you can explore the museum at your own pace. The exhibits are spread across three floors, with displays ranging from personal artefacts and photographs to interactive exhibits that allow you to trace your own family's immigration history. A highlight of the visit is the Wall of Honour, where visitors can see the names of those who passed through Ellis Island.

The museum is open from 9:00 AM to 5:00 PM, with the last entry at 4:15 PM. Expect to spend at least two hours exploring the exhibits and taking in the powerful stories of those who helped build the nation. The visit is both educational and moving, offering a unique perspective on the history of immigration in the United States.

Federal Hall National Memorial

Federal Hall, located at 26 Wall Street in the Financial District, is a significant site in American history. It was here that George Washington took the oath of office as the first President of the United States in 1789 and where the first Congress met, establishing many of the foundations of the new nation. The building you see today is a reconstruction, completed in 1842, on the site of the original Federal Hall.

The memorial is open Monday through Friday from 9:00 AM to 5:00 PM, and admission is free. It's easily accessible via the subway, with the 2, 3, 4, 5, J, and Z lines all stopping nearby at Wall Street. The area is also well served by buses and taxis.

Inside, you'll find exhibits on the early history of the United States, including the first inauguration and the creation of the Bill of Rights. The rotunda, with its grand architecture, is a highlight, and the basement holds the original stone where Washington stood during his inauguration. Federal Hall is a must-visit for history enthusiasts and those interested in the early days of American democracy.

The African Burial Ground National Monument

The African Burial Ground National Monument is a significant and sacred site located in Lower Manhattan. Discovered in 1991 during construction, this burial ground dates back to the 17th and 18th centuries and is the final resting place for over 15,000 free and enslaved Africans. The monument and museum honour their memory and provide an important reflection on the contributions and struggles of African Americans in the early history of New York.

The monument is located at 290 Broadway and is accessible by the A, C, J, Z, 2, 3, 4, and 5 subway lines, stopping at Chambers Street or Brooklyn Bridge-City Hall. It is open Tuesday through Saturday from 9:00 AM to 5:00 PM, with free admission.

Visitors can explore the outdoor monument, which includes a symbolic Ancestral Chamber, and the indoor museum that offers detailed exhibits on the burial ground's history and the lives of those interred there. It's a deeply moving experience that sheds light on a lesser-known part of New York's past.

These historic landmarks and monuments offer a window into the rich and complex history of New York City. Whether you're crossing the Brooklyn Bridge, tracing your roots at Ellis Island, standing where George Washington once stood, or reflecting at the African Burial Ground, each site provides a unique and profound connection to the city's past.

Museums and Galleries

New York City is home to some of the world's most renowned museums and galleries, each offering a rich cultural experience that reflects the city's diverse history and artistic innovation. From world-class art collections to immersive historical exhibits, these institutions are essential stops for anyone looking to explore the cultural heart of the city.

The Metropolitan Museum of Art (The Met)

The Metropolitan Museum of Art, commonly known as The Met, is one of the largest and most comprehensive art museums in the world. It houses over 2 million works of art spanning 5,000 years, offering visitors an unparalleled glimpse into various cultures and time periods. From ancient Egyptian artefacts to modern American paintings, The Met's vast collection provides something for everyone.

Scan the Qr code to book The Metropolitan Museum of Art

Located at 1000 Fifth Avenue along the eastern edge of Central Park, The Met is easily accessible by public transportation. The 4, 5, or 6 trains will take you to 86th Street, where it's just a short walk west to the museum. Alternatively, the M1, M2, M3, or M4 buses run along Fifth Avenue and stop directly in front of the museum.

The museum is open daily, except for Wednesdays, from 10:00 AM to 5:00 PM, with extended hours on Fridays and Saturdays until 9:00 PM. Admission is suggested at $49 for adults, $45 for seniors, and $39 for youths, but New York State residents and students from New Jersey and Connecticut can pay what they wish.

Inside, visitors are encouraged to explore the museum's different wings, which are organised by geographical regions and historical periods. Special exhibitions often rotate throughout the year, offering fresh and dynamic content for repeat visitors. The museum also hosts various educational programs, lectures, and tours, making it a valuable resource for learning.

The Met's rooftop garden, open seasonally, offers stunning views of Central Park and the city skyline, along with rotating art installations. The museum also features several dining options, including the elegant Dining Room, which offers a refined atmosphere with views of the park, and the Met Cafeteria for a more casual dining experience.

The Museum of Modern Art (MoMA)

The Museum of Modern Art, or MoMA, is one of the most influential modern art museums in the world. Founded in 1929, MoMA's collection includes works by some of the most iconic artists of the 20th and 21st centuries, such as Vincent van Gogh, Pablo Picasso, and Andy Warhol. The museum's galleries feature everything from paintings and sculptures to film, photography, and design.

Scan the Qr code to book The Museum of Modern Art

MoMA is located at 11 West 53rd Street, between Fifth and Sixth Avenues in Midtown Manhattan. It's easily accessible by the B, D, F, and M subway lines at the 47-50th Streets-Rockefeller Centre station or the E and M lines at Fifth Avenue/53rd Street.

The museum is open daily from 10:30 AM to 5:30 PM, with extended hours on Fridays until 8:00 PM. Admission is about $30 for adults, while children under 16 can enter for free.

Visitors can expect a dynamic and immersive experience, with galleries that explore different movements in modern art, from Surrealism to Abstract Expressionism. MoMA also frequently hosts temporary exhibitions, showcasing contemporary artists and thematic installations.

The museum's Sculpture Garden is a tranquil outdoor space where visitors can enjoy works by artists like Alexander Calder and Isamu Noguchi. MoMA also offers a variety of services, including guided tours, audio guides, and a range of educational programs. The MoMA Store is a popular destination for unique art-inspired gifts and books.

The American Museum of Natural History

The American Museum of Natural History is one of the largest and most celebrated museums in the world, known for its impressive collections that span the natural world. From dinosaur fossils to meteorites, the museum offers a comprehensive exploration of the planet's history and the life that inhabits it.

Located at Central Park West and 79th Street, the museum is easily accessible via the B or C subway lines to 81st Street—Museum of Natural History, or by the 1 train to 79th Street, followed by a short walk.

The museum is open daily from 10:00 AM to 5:30 PM. General admission is suggested at $28 for adults, $22 for seniors, and $16 for children, though you can pay what you wish for entry. Special exhibitions, like the Hayden Planetarium Space Show, require additional tickets.

Visitors can explore a wide range of exhibits, including the famous Hall of Dinosaurs, the Hall of Ocean Life, and the

Hall of Human Origins. The museum is also home to the Rose Centre for Earth and Space, which features the Hayden Planetarium, offering an incredible journey through the cosmos.

Expect to spend several hours exploring the museum, as it covers a vast area with many different sections. Educational programs, guided tours, and interactive exhibits make it a favourite for families and school groups. The museum also features several dining options, including the Food Court and the Café on One, where you can take a break during your visit.

The Whitney Museum of American Art

The Whitney Museum of American Art, commonly known as the Whitney, is dedicated to contemporary American art. It was founded in 1930 by Gertrude Vanderbilt Whitney, a prominent sculptor and patron of the arts. The museum's collection focusses on 20th and 21st-century American artists, showcasing a diverse range of styles and mediums.

Located at 99 Gansevoort Street in the Meatpacking District, the Whitney is easily accessible by the A, C, E, and L subway lines to 14th Street/Eighth Avenue. It's also a short walk from the High Line, making it an ideal stop while exploring the neighbourhood.

The museum is open Thursday through Monday, from 10:30 AM to 6:00 PM, with extended hours until 10:00 PM on Fridays and Saturdays. Admission is about $30 for adults, $24 for seniors, and free for those 18 and under.

Inside, visitors can explore galleries that showcase rotating exhibitions as well as the museum's permanent collection, which includes works by artists like Edward Hopper, Georgia O'Keeffe, and Alexander Calder. The museum's design, by architect Renzo Piano, features open and airy spaces that allow for an immersive art experience.

The Whitney's outdoor terraces offer stunning views of the Hudson River and the surrounding cityscape, providing a perfect backdrop for the museum's sculptures. The museum also hosts a variety of educational programs, lectures, and events, making it a vibrant hub for contemporary art lovers.

The museum's restaurant, Untitled, offers a seasonally inspired menu, while the Studio Café on the eighth floor provides a more casual dining option with spectacular views.

New York City's museums and galleries offer an incredible journey through art, history, and science, providing experiences that are both enriching and entertaining. These cultural institutions are essential stops on any visit to the city.

Theatres and Performance Venues

New York City is a global hub for theatre and live performances, offering a diverse range of venues where both iconic productions and experimental performances come to life. From Broadway's glitzy stages to intimate off-Broadway theatres, the city's performance venues are as much a part of its cultural fabric as its towering skyscrapers.

Broadway Theatres

Broadway is synonymous with world-class theater. Located in the heart of Midtown Manhattan, Broadway is home to 41 professional theatres, each offering a variety of performances from timeless classics to groundbreaking new productions. A Broadway show is an essential New York experience, providing entertainment that ranges from lavish musicals to compelling dramas.

Most Broadway theatres are concentrated around Times Square, making them easily accessible by the N, Q, R, S, W, 1, 2, 3, 7, A, C, and E subway lines. The theatres are within walking distance of each other, and Times Square is a central hub for buses and taxis as well.

Showtimes typically run in the evening from 7:00 PM to 8:00 PM, with matinee performances on Wednesdays, Saturdays, and Sundays. Tickets can range from $50 to $300 or more, depending on the show and seating, but discount tickets are often available at the TKTS booth in Times Square or through various online platforms.

Visitors can expect a polished and immersive theatrical experience with state-of-the-art production values, talented performers, and often elaborate stage designs. It's recommended to arrive at least 30 minutes before the show starts to find your seat and settle in. While formal attire is not required, many theatregoers choose to dress smartly, especially for evening performances.

During intermission, theatres usually offer concessions, and many have small bars where you can enjoy a drink. Photography and recording are strictly prohibited during performances, and audiences are expected to remain seated and quiet to fully enjoy the show.

Lincoln Centre for the Performing Arts

Lincoln Centre is one of the most prestigious cultural institutions in the world, encompassing multiple performance venues, including the Metropolitan Opera House, David Geffen Hall (home of the New York Philharmonic), and the David H. Koch Theatre (home to the New York City Ballet). Lincoln Centre hosts a wide range of performances, from opera and ballet to classical music concerts and theatre.

Located at 10 Lincoln Centre Plaza, between West 62nd and 65th Streets and Columbus and Amsterdam Avenues, the centre is easily accessible by the 1 subway line at the 66th Street-Lincoln Centre station. It's also served by several bus lines, and taxis are plentiful in the area.

Performances at Lincoln Centre vary widely in terms of timing and price. Opera and ballet performances can start as early as 7:00 PM, with matinees in the afternoon. Ticket prices range from $30 to several hundred dollars, depending on the performance and seating.

Expect a sophisticated atmosphere with world-class performances by leading artists. Lincoln Centre is known for its grand, modern architecture and elegant interiors, which add to the overall experience. Many performances are accompanied by surtitles (translated captions) for operas or spoken word, enhancing accessibility for international audiences.

The centre offers several dining options, from casual cafes to fine dining restaurants, allowing visitors to enjoy a meal before or after the show. It's recommended to book tickets in advance, especially for popular performances, as they often sell out.

Radio City Music Hall

Radio City Music Hall, known as the "Showplace of the Nation," is an iconic entertainment venue located in Rockefeller Center. Opened in 1932, it has hosted a wide variety of performances, including concerts, stage shows, and film premieres. Its most famous production is the annual Radio City Christmas Spectacular, featuring the legendary Rockettes.

Radio City Music Hall is located at 1260 Avenue of the Americas (Sixth Avenue) between 50th and 51st Streets. It's easily accessible by the B, D, F, and M subway lines to 47-50 Streets-Rockefeller Centre or the 1 train to 50th Street.

Showtimes vary depending on the event, but performances typically begin in the evening, with matinees for certain shows, such as the Christmas Spectacular. Ticket prices range from $50 to $150, with premium seating available at higher rates.

Visitors can expect a grand and nostalgic atmosphere, with Art Deco design elements and a large seating capacity. The stage is one of the largest in the world, allowing for elaborate and visually stunning productions. Before the show, visitors can explore the historic theatre's lobby, which features beautiful murals and a grand staircase.

Radio City offers guided tours that provide a behind-the-scenes look at the theatre's history and architecture, including access to the stage and dressing rooms. These tours are a great way to enhance your experience and learn more about one of New York's most iconic performance venues.

New York City's theatres and performance venues offer a rich and diverse cultural experience that's unmatched anywhere else. Each venue has its own unique character and charm, providing unforgettable entertainment that reflects the city's dynamic spirit.

Parks

New York City is known for its iconic parks, which offer a green escape from the urban landscape. These parks are more than just open spaces; they are cultural hubs, gathering places, and sites of natural beauty that play a vital role in the city's life.

Central Park

Central Park is perhaps the most famous urban park in the world, spanning 843 acres in the heart of Manhattan. Designed by Frederick Law Olmsted and Calvert Vaux, it opened in 1858 and offers a wide variety of activities and landscapes, including rolling meadows, wooded areas, and water bodies. The park is a haven for both relaxation and recreation, drawing millions of visitors each year.

Located between 59th and 110th Streets, bordered by Fifth Avenue to the east and Central Park West to the west, Central Park is easily accessible from almost anywhere in Manhattan. Multiple subway lines serve the park: the A, B,

C, D, and 1 trains stop at 59th Street-Columbus Circle, while the 4, 5, and 6 trains stop at 59th Street, and the N, R, and Q trains also stop near the park.

The park is open daily from 6:00 AM to 1:00 AM, offering ample time to explore its vast grounds. There's no entry fee, making it a budget-friendly option for both tourists and locals. As you stroll through the park, you can enjoy famous attractions like the Bethesda Terrace, the Bow Bridge, and the Central Park Zoo. The park also offers numerous recreational activities, including boating on the lake, cycling, ice skating in the winter, and even horse-drawn carriage rides.

Central Park is a cultural hub, hosting free performances by the New York Philharmonic and Shakespeare in the Park during the summer months. The park's rules are straightforward: respect the environment by not littering, keep dogs on a leash except in designated areas, and avoid amplified sound or alcohol consumption without a permit.

Bryant Park

Bryant Park is a vibrant green space located in Midtown Manhattan, between 40th and 42nd Streets and Fifth and Sixth Avenues. It's a relatively small park, covering 9.6 acres, but it's packed with activities and cultural events that make it a popular destination for both locals and tourists.

The park is easily accessible by subway, with the B, D, F, and M trains stopping at 42nd Street-Bryant Park and the 7 train stopping at 5th Avenue. It's also within walking distance of many of Midtown's attractions, including the

New York Public Library, which borders the park to the east.

Bryant Park is open daily from 7:00 AM to 10:00 PM, with extended hours during special events. It offers a variety of free activities, from outdoor movie nights in the summer to ice skating at the Winter Village during the holiday season. The park is also known for its well-maintained gardens, outdoor reading room, and historic carousel.

While in the park, you can enjoy a meal at one of its many outdoor cafés or bring your own food for a picnic on the lawn. The park's rules encourage visitors to relax and enjoy the space responsibly, with guidelines similar to Central Park's, including no smoking, no amplified sound, and keeping pets on a leash.

Prospect Park

Prospect Park is the crown jewel of Brooklyn, designed by the same team behind Central Park. Spanning 526 acres, it offers a tranquil escape with its rolling meadows, dense forests, and a large lake. The park is home to several attractions, including the Prospect Park Zoo, the Brooklyn Botanic Garden, and the historic Lefferts House.

Located in the heart of Brooklyn, Prospect Park is bordered by Flatbush Avenue, Eastern Parkway, Prospect Park West, and Parkside Avenue. It's accessible by the B, Q, and S trains to Prospect Park station, the 2, 3 trains to Grand Army Plaza, and the F, G trains to 15th Street-Prospect Park.

The park is open daily from 5:00 AM to 1:00 AM, offering a wide range of activities throughout the day. Visitors can enjoy birdwatching in the Ravine, boating on the lake, or attending free concerts at the Bandshell during the summer. The park also offers numerous sports facilities, including tennis courts, baseball fields, and cycling paths.

Prospect Park is known for its community-orientated events, such as farmers' markets and cultural festivals. The park's rules emphasise respect for nature and fellow visitors, with restrictions on littering, smoking, and alcohol consumption. Dogs are welcome but must be leashed except in designated off-leash areas.

The High Line

The High Line is a unique urban park built on a historic elevated rail line on Manhattan's West Side. Stretching 1.45 miles from Gansevoort Street in the Meatpacking District to 34th Street, the park offers stunning views of the city and the Hudson River. It's a prime example of urban renewal, transforming an abandoned railway into a green space that blends art, nature, and design.

The High Line is accessible from several points along its route, with entrances at Gansevoort Street, 14th Street, 23rd Street, and 34th Street. The closest subway stations are the A, C, and E trains at 14th Street-Eighth Avenue or the 7 train at Hudson Yards.

The park is open daily, with seasonal hours varying from 7:00 AM to 10:00 PM in the summer and 7:00 AM to 7:00 PM in the winter. Admission is free, and visitors can enjoy leisurely walks along the landscaped pathways, which are dotted with public art installations, gardens, and seating areas.

The High Line offers various programs and tours, often focussing on its history, design, and the surrounding neighbourhoods. Visitors are encouraged to stay on the designated paths, respect the plant life, and refrain from smoking or bringing pets into the park.

These parks in New York City are essential stops for anyone looking to experience the city beyond its skyscrapers.

Walking Tours

Walking tours are a fantastic way to explore New York City, offering an immersive experience that allows you to truly connect with the city's history, culture, and neighborhoods.

Walking tours in New York City are guided experiences that take you through various parts of the city on foot, led by knowledgeable guides who provide in-depth commentary on the sites you visit. These tours typically last between one and three hours and cover a variety of themes, from historical explorations to food tasting journeys, ghost stories, and art walks. The tours are designed to be engaging and informative, offering both tourists and locals a deeper understanding of the city's rich tapestry.

How to Get There

Walking tours are offered in almost every neighbourhood of New York City, with popular starting points in areas like Times Square, Central Park, SoHo, and the Lower East Side. Most tours meet at easily accessible landmarks or subway stations. For example, a tour of Central Park might start at the Columbus Circle entrance, accessible by the A, B, C, D, and 1 subway lines. A Greenwich Village tour could begin at Washington Square Park, easily reached by the A, C, E, B, D, F, M, or R trains.

Opening Hours and Booking

Tours are typically available year-round, with multiple departures each day. Morning tours are common, but many operators also offer afternoon and evening tours to accommodate different schedules. Booking in advance is recommended, especially for popular tours, but many companies also accept walk-up participants if space allows. You can book tours through the company's website, travel agencies, or platforms like TripAdvisor and Viator.

Cost and Budget

The cost of walking tours in New York City can vary widely. Basic tours might start at $20 per person, while more specialised or private tours can cost upwards of $50 to $100. Some companies offer free or pay-what-you-wish tours, where you're encouraged to tip the guide based on your experience. No matter your budget, there's a walking tour that fits your needs.

During a walking tour, expect to cover between one and three miles, depending on the tour. You'll visit key landmarks and lesser-known spots, with your guide sharing historical facts, anecdotes, and insider tips along the way. Some tours include stops at local businesses, like cafes or bakeries, where you can sample food or beverages as part of the experience. Others might involve interactive elements, such as re-enacting historical events or solving puzzles related to the tour theme.

It's important to arrive on time, as tours generally start promptly. Wear comfortable walking shoes and dress appropriately for the weather as tours proceed, rain or shine. Many tours involve standing and walking for extended periods, so be prepared for a moderate amount of physical activity. Guides usually appreciate tips if you enjoyed the tour, especially on pay-what-you-wish tours where tips are the main source of income for the guide.

Most walking tours offer basic amenities like restroom breaks or opportunities to purchase refreshments. Some tours provide headphones to ensure you can hear the guide clearly in noisy environments. It's a good idea to carry water, especially during warmer months, and a small backpack for any personal items.

Walking tours often provide a more intimate look at the city, uncovering hidden gems and stories that you might miss on a bus or bike tour.

Walking tours are an excellent way to dive deep into New York City's neighbourhoods, learn about its history, and engage with the local culture. They offer flexibility, a range of topics to explore, and the opportunity to see the city from a new perspective, all while enjoying the simple pleasure of a walk through one of the world's most dynamic cities.

Hidden Gems

New York City is full of famous landmarks, but it also harbours some lesser-known treasures that offer a more intimate, off-the-beaten-path experience. These hidden gems are beloved by locals and offer a unique way to explore the city away from the typical tourist crowds.

The Elevated Acre

The Elevated Acre is a secluded urban park located in the Financial District. This hidden green space offers a peaceful retreat with stunning views of the East River and the Brooklyn Bridge. It's a perfect spot for a quiet lunch or simply to unwind with a book.

Located at 55 Water Street, the park is tucked away on a raised platform, accessible by an escalator from the street level. The nearest subway station is Whitehall Street-South Ferry, served by the N and R trains. The 2, 3, 4, 5, and J trains also stop nearby at Wall Street.

The park is open daily from 8:00 AM to 8:00 PM, with no entrance fee, making it an affordable and accessible escape from the hustle and bustle of the city. Visitors can enjoy the well-maintained lawns, a small amphitheatre, and beautifully landscaped gardens. It's a popular spot for nearby office workers, but tourists can also appreciate its tranquilly and the panoramic views of the river.

The Elevated Acre is a great place to relax, take in the views, and enjoy a quieter side of New York. Bring your own refreshments, as there are no cafes or shops directly in the park, and take advantage of this peaceful urban oasis.

Green-Wood Cemetery

Greenwood Cemetery in Brooklyn is a historic cemetery that doubles as a stunning park, filled with rolling hills, beautiful trees, and impressive sculptures. Founded in 1838, it's the final resting place of many famous New Yorkers, including artist Jean-Michel Basquiat and composer Leonard Bernstein.

Located at 500 25th Street in Brooklyn, Greenwood is easily accessible by the D, N, and R trains to 25th Street station, followed by a short walk. The cemetery is open daily from 8:00 AM to 5:00 PM, and entrance is free.

Visitors can expect a serene and contemplative atmosphere, with winding paths that lead past ornate mausoleums, Gothic arches, and ponds. The cemetery offers guided tours that explore its history, art, and architecture. Additionally, it's a popular spot for birdwatching and photography, with its natural beauty providing a striking backdrop.

Greenwood Cemetery is not just a place to pay respects; it's a beautiful park that offers a unique perspective on the city's history. Be mindful of the solemn nature of the site, and take time to appreciate both the history and the tranquilly of this hidden gem.

The Cloisters

The Cloisters is a branch of the Metropolitan Museum of Art, dedicated to the art and architecture of mediaeval Europe. Located in Fort Tryon Park in Upper Manhattan, this museum is a hidden treasure that transports visitors to a different time and place with its stunning collection of mediaeval art and its beautiful, monastery-like setting.

The Cloisters is located at 99 Margaret Corbin Drive in Fort Tryon Park. The A train to 190th Street will bring you closest, followed by a scenic walk through the park. The museum is open daily from 10:00 AM to 4:30 PM, with extended hours during the summer.

Admission is included with The Met's general ticket, which is $30 for adults, $22 for seniors, and $17 for students. Pay-what-you-wish admission is available for New York State residents.

Inside, visitors can explore reconstructed mediaeval chapels, tapestries, and gardens that reflect the art and culture of the Middle Ages. The building itself, constructed from architectural elements from European monasteries, is as much a part of the experience as the art it houses. Expect a peaceful and reflective environment, with fewer crowds than The Met's main location.

The Cloisters offers a unique escape into another era, with beautifully curated exhibits and a tranquil setting that feels far removed from the city's hustle and bustle. It's a must-visit for art lovers and those looking to explore a different side of New York's cultural offerings.

The Noguchi Museum

The Noguchi Museum in Queens is dedicated to the works of Japanese-American sculptor Isamu Noguchi. Tucked away in the Astoria neighbourhood, this museum offers a quiet, contemplative space to appreciate Noguchi's minimalist sculptures and designs.

Located at 9-01 33rd Road in Long Island City, Queens, the museum is a bit off the typical tourist path but easily reachable by the N or W trains to Broadway station, followed by a short walk.

The museum is open Wednesday through Sunday, from 11:00 AM to 6:00 PM. Admission is $12 for adults, $6 for seniors and students, and free for children under 12. The museum also offers free admission on the first Friday of each month.

Visitors can expect a serene atmosphere, with both indoor galleries and an outdoor sculpture garden. The museum's design reflects Noguchi's philosophy of art as an integral part of daily life, and the spaces are thoughtfully arranged to create a dialogue between the artworks and the environment.

The Noguchi Museum offers a peaceful retreat for those interested in modern art and design. It's a place to slow down, reflect, and immerse yourself in the artist's vision. The museum's shop is also worth a visit, offering a selection of Noguchi-inspired items and unique gifts.

These hidden gems offer a more intimate and local experience of New York City, away from the typical tourist spots. Each provides a unique perspective on the city's culture, history, and natural beauty, making them well worth a visit for those looking to explore beyond the well-trodden paths.

Exploring New York City's top attractions is an unforgettable experience that captures the essence of this metropolis. As you reflect on your adventures, you'll find that the city's charm lies in its ability to surprise and inspire at every turn.

Chapter 6

New York City for Different Travellers

New York City is a destination that offers something for every kind of traveler. You'll see how different visitors can experience the city in ways that suit their preferences and interests.

NYC for Solo Travellers

Things to Do as a Solo Traveler

New York City is a playground for solo travellers, offering a variety of activities that are best enjoyed independently.

The Metropolitan Museum of Art (The Met)

Wander through vast galleries at your own pace, immersing yourself in art from different cultures and time periods.

Central Park

Enjoy a peaceful stroll, rent a bike, or simply relax on a bench and people-watch.

Cost is free, with optional rentals or tours.

The High Line

A walk along this elevated park offers stunning views of the city, perfect for solo exploration.

Cost is free.

Places for Solo Exploration

New York City's neighbourhoods are brimming with character, and exploring them on your own allows you to truly soak in their unique atmospheres.

Lower East Side

Check out street art, eclectic shops, and hidden cafes.

Location is between Bowery and East River, Manhattan.

It's free to explore, but you can budget for shopping or dining.

Greenwich Village

Visit the tree-lined streets, independent bookshops, and historic landmarks like the Stonewall Inn.

Location is west of Broadway, between 14th Street and Houston Street, Manhattan.

It's free to explore, but you can budget for cafes or stores.

DUMBO, Brooklyn

Capture iconic views of the Brooklyn Bridge and explore local art galleries.

You can budget for galleries or cafes.

Joining Tours and Group Activities

If you're looking to meet fellow travellers, joining a tour or group activity is a great option. They include

Foods of NY Tours

Budget is $50-$75 per tour.

Central Park Bike Tour

Budget is $50-$60.

Eataly Cooking Classes

Budget is $85-$125 per class.

Solo Dining

New York City offers a plethora of dining options perfect for solo travellers, especially at spots with communal seating.

Eataly

Location: 200 Fifth Avenue, Manhattan.

Budget: $15-$30 for meals.

Momofuku Noodle Bar

Location: 171 First Avenue, Manhattan.

Budget: $15-$25.

Russ & Daughters Café

Location: 127 Orchard Street, Manhattan.

Budget: $20-$40.

Safety Tips for Solo Travellers

New York City is generally safe, but solo travellers should always stay vigilant. Stick to well-lit and busy areas, especially at night. Use rideshare services for late-night transport, and avoid empty subway cars. Be mindful of your belongings, particularly in crowded areas like Times Square or subway stations. Sharing your itinerary with a trusted person and checking in regularly is also a good practice. Trust your instincts, and don't hesitate to ask for help if you ever feel uncomfortable.

By following these tips and embracing the city's vibrant energy, solo travellers can enjoy an unforgettable and enriching experience in New York City.

NYC for Couples

Romantic Walks

New York City offers some of the most picturesque spots for couples looking to enjoy a romantic stroll. These locations provide the perfect backdrop for intimate moments and scenic views.

The High Line

This elevated park on Manhattan's West Side is a beautiful place for a romantic walk. The park stretches 1.45 miles from Gansevoort Street to 34th Street, offering gardens, art installations, and views of the Hudson River.

Budget: Free.

Brooklyn Promenade

The Brooklyn Promenade offers stunning views of the Manhattan skyline, the Statue of Liberty, and the Brooklyn Bridge. It's a favourite spot for couples to take in the sunset or enjoy a quiet moment.

Location: Montague Street, Brooklyn Heights.

Budget:Free.

Central Park's Bow Bridge

Bow Bridge is one of Central Park's most romantic spots, offering a picturesque setting over the lake. It's a popular spot for couples to take a leisurely walk or even propose.

Location: Central Park, Manhattan.

Budget: Free.

Rooftop Bars and Restaurants

New York City is known for its stunning rooftop bars and restaurants, offering couples a chance to enjoy each other's company while taking in panoramic views of the city.

230 Fifth Rooftop Bar

One of the largest rooftop bars in NYC, 230 Fifth offers breathtaking views of the Empire State Building and the Manhattan skyline.

Location: 230 Fifth Avenue, Manhattan.

Budget: Drinks typically range from $15-$25.

The Press Lounge

Located atop the Ink48 Hotel, The Press Lounge is known for its sophisticated atmosphere and stunning views of the Hudson River and Midtown Manhattan.

Location: 653 11th Avenue, Manhattan.

Budget: Cocktails range from $18-$25.

Westlight

Situated in Williamsburg, Brooklyn, Westlight offers 360-degree views of Manhattan from across the river, combined with a creative cocktail menu.

Location: 111 North 12th Street, Brooklyn.

Budget: Cocktails around $20.

Couples' Activities

Couples looking to share unique experiences will find plenty of activities that cater to two.

Tandem Bike Rides in Central Park

Exploring Central Park on a tandem bike is a fun and active way to see the park together.

Location: Central Park, Manhattan.

Budget: Rentals start around $40 per hour.

Statue of Liberty & Ellis Island Cruise

A cruise to the Statue of Liberty and Ellis Island offers couples a chance to enjoy iconic sights while sharing a historical experience.

Location: Departures from Battery Park, Manhattan.

Budget: $25-$30 per person.

Wine Tasting at City Winery

City Winery offers a unique experience where couples can enjoy a wine tasting while overlooking the Hudson River.

Location: 25 11th Avenue, Manhattan.

Budget: Tasting flights range from $20-$40.

Romantic Spots for Sunset Views

Sunset in New York City can be a magical experience, and there are several spots that are particularly well-suited for couples to enjoy together.

Top of the Rock

The observation deck at the Rockefeller Centre offers some of the best sunset views in the city, with a perfect vantage point over Central Park and Midtown Manhattan.

Location 30 Rockefeller Plaza, Manhattan.

Budget: $40-$60 per person.

Gantry Plaza State Park

Located in Long Island City, this park offers unobstructed views of the Manhattan skyline, making it a perfect spot for watching the sunset.

Location: 4-44 47th Road, Long Island City, Queens.

Budget: Free.

One World Observatory

Located at the top of the One World Trade Centre, this observatory provides breathtaking views of the entire city, particularly at sunset.

Location: 117 West Street, Manhattan.

Budget: $38-$58 per person.

NYC offers countless opportunities for couples to create unforgettable memories together. The city's diverse options cater to all kinds of couples, ensuring a rich and fulfilling experience.

Family-Friendly Activities

Kid-Friendly Museums and Interactive Exhibits

New York City is home to a number of museums that cater specifically to children, offering interactive exhibits that engage young minds and make learning fun.

American Museum of Natural History

Known for its incredible dinosaur exhibits, the museum also features the Discovery Room, where kids can touch fossils, explore drawers of specimens, and more.

Children's Museum of Manhattan (CMOM)

This museum offers a variety of interactive exhibits designed to stimulate learning and creativity in young children.

Location: 212 West 83rd Street, Manhattan.

Budget: $15 per person; free for children under 12 months.

New York Hall of Science

Located in Queens, this museum offers more than 450 interactive exhibits on science, technology, engineering, and math.

Location: 47-01 111th Street, Queens.

Budget: $16 for adults, $13 for children; free admission on Fridays and Sundays.

Zoos and Aquariums

New York City's zoos and aquariums offer families an exciting way to learn about wildlife and marine life while enjoying a day outdoors.

Bronx Zoo

One of the largest zoos in the world, the Bronx Zoo offers a vast array of animals and exhibits, including the Congo Gorilla Forest and the Butterfly Garden.

Central Park Zoo

Located in the heart of Central Park, this smaller zoo is perfect for younger children, with exhibits like the penguin habitat and the snow leopard enclosure.

New York Aquarium

Situated on Coney Island, this aquarium features exhibits on marine life, including sharks, sea otters, and a vibrant coral reef.

Theme Parks and Fun Zones

For a day of thrills and fun, New York City offers several theme parks and entertainment zones that are perfect for families.

Luna Park at Coney Island

This historic amusement park offers classic rides like the Cyclone roller coaster, as well as newer attractions and games.

Adventurers Amusement Park

Located in Brooklyn, this smaller amusement park is great for younger kids, with rides like the carousel and bumper cars.

Governor's Island

Though not a traditional theme park, Governor's Island offers activities like mini-golf, playgrounds, and bike rentals, making it a great spot for family fun.

Places for Family Picnics and Outdoor Fun

New York City's parks offer the perfect settings for family picnics, outdoor games, and other recreational activities.

Central Park

The Great Lawn and Sheep Meadow are ideal spots for picnics, while the park also offers playgrounds, boat rentals, and open spaces for games.

Prospect Park

Brooklyn's sprawling park features barbecue areas, playgrounds, and the Prospect Park Zoo, making it a favourite for family outings.

Brooklyn Bridge Park

Located along the East River, this park offers picnic tables, playgrounds, and a stunning view of the Manhattan skyline.

Tips for Visiting NYC with Babies and Toddlers

Travelling with young children in New York City can be a fun and rewarding experience with a bit of preparation. Here are some tips to ensure a smooth visit:

Stroller-Friendly Areas

Many of the city's parks, such as Central Park and the High Line, are stroller-friendly and offer plenty of space for little ones to roam.

Public Transportation

The subway is the quickest way to get around, but not all stations have elevators. Consider using buses or taxis with car seats for more convenience.

Restrooms and Changing Areas

Look for family restrooms in museums, larger stores, and shopping centers. The American Museum of Natural History and the Children's Museum of Manhattan are particularly well-equipped for families.

NYC for First-Time Visitors

Must-Know Tips for a Smooth Visit

For first-time visitors to New York City, understanding how to navigate the city is key to having a successful trip. One of the most important things to know is that New York is vast and densely populated, so planning ahead is crucial. The subway is the quickest and most efficient way to get around, and it's worth familiarising yourself with the subway map before you arrive. Download a reliable transit app like Citymapper or Google Maps, which can help you navigate the subway and bus systems with ease.

When visiting popular attractions like the Statue of Liberty or the Empire State Building, buy your tickets online in advance to avoid long lines. Many attractions also offer timed-entry tickets, which can save you hours of waiting. Remember that New York is a walking city, so bring comfortable shoes and be prepared to walk several miles each day. Also, keep in mind that the weather can be unpredictable, so packing layers is always a good idea.

Avoiding Common Tourist Mistakes

One common mistake first-time visitors make is trying to do too much in too little time. New York City has an overwhelming amount of things to see and do, so it's better to focus on a few key attractions each day rather than trying to cram everything in. This allows you to enjoy each experience without feeling rushed.

Another mistake is eating at the first restaurant you see, especially in tourist-heavy areas like Times Square. While there are some good options, many restaurants in these areas are overpriced and underwhelming. Instead, venture a little further out to find local favorites. Apps like Yelp and OpenTable can help you discover well-reviewed restaurants that are popular with locals.

How to Make the Most of Your NYC Experience

To truly make the most of your visit to New York City, consider exploring beyond the typical tourist spots. While Times Square and Central Park are must-sees, neighbourhoods like the Lower East Side, Williamsburg in Brooklyn, and Harlem offer unique cultural experiences, diverse food scenes, and a chance to see the city from a local's perspective.

Consider taking a walking tour or joining a food tour to gain deeper insights into the city's history and culture. The New York Public Library offers free tours of its main branch, which is an architectural marvel, and the Brooklyn Brewery offers affordable tours that include tastings.

Also, don't be afraid to take in a Broadway show, but remember that off-Broadway and local theatre productions can be just as impressive and often more affordable. TKTS booths in Times Square and other locations offer discounted same-day tickets to many Broadway and off-Broadway shows.

Safety Tips and Local Scams to Watch Out For

New York City is generally safe for tourists, but like any large city, it's important to stay aware of your surroundings. Stick to well-lit and populated areas, especially at night, and avoid deserted streets. When using the subway, be cautious of your belongings, particularly in crowded stations and trains.

Be wary of common scams targeting tourists. For example, don't buy tickets from street vendors or accept "free" CDs from people who then demand money. In popular areas like Times Square, avoid costumed characters who may charge for photos. Stick to official ticket vendors and attractions, and if something feels off, trust your instincts.

Best Apps and Resources for Visitors

Having the right apps and resources can make your visit to New York City much smoother and more enjoyable.

Citymapper

A highly recommended app for navigating the city's public transportation, offering real-time updates on subway and bus routes.

OpenTable

Ideal for making restaurant reservations, especially for popular dining spots that may fill up quickly.

TripAdvisor

Useful for finding reviews on attractions, restaurants, and hotels, as well as discovering lesser-known spots recommended by other travellers.

TodayTix

A great resource for finding discounted theatre tickets, including Broadway and off-Broadway shows.

New York City Official Guide

The city's official tourism website offers a wealth of information on events, attractions, and helpful tips for visitors.

By planning ahead, avoiding common pitfalls, and using the right resources, first-time visitors to New York City can have a memorable and enjoyable experience, filled with the unique excitement that the city has to offer.

NYC for the Adventurous

Activities for the Adventurous

New York City isn't just about iconic landmarks and cultural attractions; it also offers a range of thrilling activities for those seeking adventure. It has plenty to satisfy your adventurous spirit.

Helicopter Rides Over the City

For an adrenaline-pumping experience, a helicopter ride over New York City offers unparalleled views of its iconic skyline. Companies like Liberty Helicopters and HeliNY provide tours that fly over landmarks such as the Statue of Liberty, Empire State Building, and Central Park.

Budget: Rides typically cost between $200-$350 per person for a 15- to 30-mminute flight.

Hot Air Balloon Rides

While not as common in the city itself, hot air balloon rides near NYC offer a peaceful yet exhilarating way to take in the surrounding landscapes. Companies like Above the Clouds offer rides just outside the city, in areas like the Hudson Valley, where you can enjoy views of rolling hills, rivers, and historic sites.

Budget: Rides range from $200-$300 per person for a one-hour flight.

Kayaking on the Hudson River

For a water-based adventure, kayaking on the Hudson River provides a unique way to experience the city. Several organisations, like the Downtown Boathouse, offer free kayaking sessions during the warmer months, allowing you to paddle along the river with views of the Manhattan skyline.

Location: Piers along the Hudson River, such as Pier 26 or Pier 96.

Budget: Free to low-cost, depending on the provider.

Urban Exploration

For those interested in urban exploration, NYC has a hidden side that includes abandoned tunnels, historic sites, and rooftop views. While some of these activities require permission or are part of guided tours, they offer a different perspective on the city's history and architecture.

Hidden Tunnels

Explore the old City Hall subway station, accessible through guided tours by the New York Transit Museum.

Budget: Tours cost around $50 per person.

Rooftop Views

For legal rooftop access, visit places like 230 Fifth Rooftop Bar or Top of the Rock. These locations offer stunning views of the skyline without the risk associated with trespassing on unauthorised rooftops. .

Budget: Entry fees or the cost of a drink, typically $15-$30.

New York City's adventurous activities cater to a variety of interests. These experiences provide unforgettable memories that go beyond the typical tourist itinerary.

NYC for Budget Travellers

New York City is often seen as an expensive destination, but with some savvy planning, budget travellers can experience much of what the city has to offer without breaking the bank.

How to Enjoy NYC on a Budget

Exploring New York City on a budget is all about making smart choices. One of the best ways to save money is by taking advantage of the many free and low-cost attractions. The city's extensive public transportation system makes it easy to get around without needing a car, and with a bit of planning, you can experience some of the best of NYC without spending a fortune.

Budget Accommodations

Finding affordable accommodations in New York City can be challenging, but not impossible. Hostels, budget hotels, and short-term apartment rentals are great options for travellers looking to save money.

HI New York City Hostel

Located on the Upper West Side, this hostel offers clean and comfortable dormitory-style rooms with a social atmosphere.

Budget: Starting at around $50 per night.

Pod 51 Hotel

This budget-friendly hotel offers compact, modern rooms in Midtown Manhattan, with a rooftop deck providing city views.

Budget: Starting at around $100 per night.

Free and Low-Cost Attractions

New York City is filled with free and low-cost attractions that allow you to experience the city's culture and history without spending much.

Central Park

One of the most iconic parks in the world, Central Park offers free entry and plenty of space to explore.

Budget: Free.

The Metropolitan Museum of Art

While the suggested admission is $30 for adults, New York State residents can pay what they wish.

The Staten Island Ferry

This free ferry ride offers stunning views of the Statue of Liberty and the Manhattan skyline, making it a great budget-friendly way to see the sights.

Budget-Friendly Dining and Shopping

New York City's diverse food scene includes plenty of budget-friendly dining options.

Joe's Pizza

Famous for its New York-style pizza, Joe's is a must-visit for budget-conscious travelers.

Location: 7 Carmine Street, Manhattan.

Budget: About $3 per slice.

Chinatown's Dumpling Spots

Chinatown is home to many inexpensive and tasty dumpling shops. Places like Prosperity Dumpling offer filling meals for just a few dollars.

Budget: $5-$10 for a meal.

For budget-friendly shopping, head to areas like Canal Street for souvenirs or Union Square's Greenmarket for fresh, local produce.

Transportation Hacks for Saving Money

New York's public transportation system is extensive and affordable, making it the best way for budget travellers to get around.

Subway and Buses

Purchase a MetroCard for unlimited weekly rides ($34 for 7 days), allowing you to explore the city without worrying about individual fares.

Bike Rentals

For an affordable and fun way to see the city, consider renting a bike. Citi Bike offers a 24-hour pass for $12, giving you access to bikes throughout the city.

Best Times to Visit for Discounts

Visiting New York City during the off-peak seasons, such as January to March or late September to early November, can save you money on accommodations and attractions.

Winter (January-March)

Fewer tourists mean lower hotel rates and shorter lines at major attractions.

Fall (late September-November)

The weather is pleasant, and while it's busier than winter, it's still more affordable than peak summer months.

By planning ahead, knowing where to find deals, and taking advantage of free attractions, budget travellers can fully enjoy all that New York City has to offer without overspending.

New York City is a place where every traveler can find something that speaks to them. Its endless variety ensures that everyone, no matter their interests or travel style, can have an unforgettable experience. By embracing what makes this city unique and exploring it in a way that suits you best, you're sure to leave with memories that will last a lifetime. The city's energy, diversity, and countless opportunities for discovery make it a destination like no other, inviting you to experience it in your own way.

CHAPTER 7

New York City with Kids

New York City offers an abundance of experiences that cater to families travelling with kids. The city is full of activities that will keep kids entertained while providing a memorable experience for the whole family.

Playgrounds and Parks

New York City is home to a variety of playgrounds and parks that cater to children of all ages, providing safe and engaging environments for play and exploration. These spots are designed with families in mind, offering a range of activities that ensure kids can burn off energy while parents enjoy the outdoor settings.

Central Park's Heckscher Playground

Heckscher Playground, located in Central Park, is the oldest and largest playground in the park, offering an expansive area for children to play. With its combination of water features, climbing structures, and sand areas, it's a favourite among locals and visitors alike.

How to Get There

The playground is easily accessible via the N, Q, R, and W trains to 59th Street-Columbus Circle or the A, B, C, D, and 1 trains to 59th Street.

Opening Hours

Central Park is open daily from 6:00 AM to 1:00 AM; playgrounds generally close at dusk.

Budget

Free.

Heckscher Playground features a variety of play areas, including a large climbing structure, water sprinklers, swings, and sandboxes. It's ideal for kids of all ages, with shaded benches for parents to relax.

Restrooms are nearby, and the park is stroller-friendly, making it convenient for families.

Brooklyn Bridge Park's Pier 6 Playgrounds

Brooklyn Bridge Park offers several themed playgrounds at Pier 6, providing an adventurous experience for kids. From water play to climbing walls, the playgrounds here are designed to spark imagination and physical activity.

How to Get There

Accessible via the 2, 3, 4, 5 trains to Borough Hall or the R train to Court Street. The NYC Ferry also stops at Brooklyn Bridge Park.

Opening Hours

Open daily from 6:00 AM to 1:00 AM, with playgrounds typically open until dusk.

Budget

Free.

Pier 6 features multiple playgrounds, including a Water Lab for cooling off on hot days, a Slide Mountain with various slides, and the Sandbox Village for younger children. The views of the Manhattan skyline add to the park's charm.

The park includes restrooms, picnic areas, and food vendors, making it easy to spend a full day exploring.

Union Square Playground

Union Square Playground is a popular spot for families in Manhattan, offering a safe and well-maintained environment for children to play in the heart of the city.

Address

16th Street & Union Square West, Manhattan.

How to Get There

The playground is located near the 14th Street-Union Square subway station, accessible via the L, N, Q, R, W, 4, 5, and 6 trains.

Opening Hours

Open daily from 6:00 AM to 1:00 AM.

Budget

Free.

This playground features modern play structures, including climbing walls, slides, and swings. It's designed for children of various ages and is surrounded by plenty of seating for parents.

The playground is close to the Union Square Greenmarket, where families can pick up fresh snacks. Restrooms are available nearby.

Tompkins Square Park Playground

Located in the East Village, Tompkins Square Park Playground is a neighbourhood favourite, offering a relaxed and welcoming space for families.

Address

East 10th Street between Avenues A and B, Manhattan.

How to Get There

Accessible via the L train to First Avenue or the 6 train to Astor Place.

Opening Hours

Open daily from 6:00 AM to midnight.

Budget

Free.

The playground includes a variety of play structures, water features, and ample seating. The park itself is known for its community events and vibrant atmosphere.

The playground is located near several family-friendly cafes and eateries, making it easy to grab a bite before or after playtime.

New York City's playgrounds and parks offer a diverse range of activities for kids. These spaces provide a great way for children to enjoy the outdoors while giving parents a chance to relax and soak in the city's vibrant energy. With plenty of amenities like restrooms, picnic areas, and nearby dining options, these playgrounds are designed to make family outings as enjoyable and stress-free as possible.

Educational Attractions

New York City is a treasure trove of educational attractions that captivate young minds while providing fun and interactive learning experiences.

American Museum of Natural History

The American Museum of Natural History is one of the most renowned science museums in the world, offering a comprehensive look at natural history, human cultures, and the universe. It is particularly famous for its dinosaur fossils, the Hall of Ocean Life, and the Hayden Planetarium.

The museum features a wide range of exhibits, from towering dinosaur skeletons to immersive dioramas depicting various ecosystems. The Hayden Planetarium offers shows that explore space and the cosmos, narrated by notable figures like Neil deGrasse Tyson.

The museum has several cafes and a gift shop, making it easy to spend a full day exploring. Guided tours are available, and the museum is stroller-friendly.

Intrepid Sea, Air & Space Museum

The Intrepid Sea, Air & Space Museum is a unique educational attraction that offers hands-on experiences related to aviation, space exploration, and maritime history. Located on the historic aircraft carrier USS Intrepid, the museum also includes the Space Shuttle Pavilion and a Concorde jet.

Address

Pier 86, W 46th Street & 12th Avenue, Manhattan.

How to Get There

Accessible by the A, C, and E trains to 42nd Street-Port Authority Bus Terminal, followed by a short walk.

Opening Hours

Open daily from 10:00 AM to 5:00 PM.

Budget

General admission is $33 for adults and $24 for children.

Expect interactive exhibits, including aircraft you can explore, space capsules, and even the chance to sit in the cockpit of a fighter jet. The museum also offers educational programs and special events for kids.

The museum has a cafe and gift shop and is fully accessible, with stroller-friendly paths and elevators.

New York Hall of Science

Located in Queens, the New York Hall of Science (NYSCI) is dedicated to making science accessible and engaging for kids. With over 450 exhibits, it covers a range of scientific disciplines, including physics, biology, and technology.

Address

47-01 111th Street, Queens.

How to Get There

Accessible by the 7 train to 111th Street or the E, F, M, and R trains to 74th Street-Broadway, followed by a bus ride.

Opening Hours

Open Wednesday through Sunday from 10:00 AM to 5:00 PM.

Budget

General admission is $16 for adults, $13 for children; free on Fridays from 2:00 PM to 5:00 PM and Sundays from 10:00 AM to 11:00 AM.

The museum features hands-on exhibits like the Design Lab, where kids can build and test their inventions, and the Sports Challenge, which combines physical activity with science learning. The outdoor science playground is a favourite, with interactive water features and climbing structures.

The museum has a cafe, and the surrounding Flushing Meadows-Corona Park is ideal for a post-visit picnic.

Bronx Zoo's Congo Gorilla Forest

While the Bronx Zoo is primarily known for its incredible collection of animals, it also offers an educational experience through exhibits like the Congo Gorilla Forest. This immersive exhibit is designed to teach visitors about gorillas and their natural habitats as well as conservation efforts.

Address

2300 Southern Boulevard, Bronx.

How to Get There

Accessible by the 2, 5 trains to West Farms Square-East Tremont Avenue, followed by a short walk.

Opening Hours

Open daily from 10:00 AM to 4:30 PM in the winter and 10:00 AM to 5:00 PM in the summer.

Budget

General admission is $41.95 for adults, $31.95 for children; free admission on Wednesdays with a suggested donation.

The Congo Gorilla Forest offers an up-close look at gorillas, along with interactive displays that educate visitors on the importance of wildlife conservation. The exhibit includes a jungle-like setting with waterfalls and lush vegetation, making it a favourite among children and adults alike.

The zoo has multiple cafes and picnic areas, as well as gift shops with educational toys and books.

These educational attractions in New York City offer a lot of fun and learning for kids. With hands-on exhibits, immersive environments, and opportunities to explore, these destinations ensure that children not only enjoy their visit but also leave with a deeper understanding of the world around them.

Child-Friendly Restaurants and Cafés

New York City is filled with family-friendly dining options that cater to both children and adults. These restaurants and cafés offer menus designed to please younger palates while providing a welcoming atmosphere for the whole family.

Ellen's Stardust Diner

Ellen's Stardust Diner is a classic American diner famous for its singing waitstaff, who entertain guests with Broadway-style performances. The lively atmosphere and kid-friendly menu make it a hit with families visiting Times Square.

Address

1650 Broadway, Manhattan.

How to Get There

Located near Times Square, accessible via the N, Q, R, W, 1, 2, 3, A, C, and E trains to 42nd Street.

Opening Hours

Open daily from 7:00 AM to 11:00 PM.

Budget

Meals range from $15-$30.

Expect classic diner fare like burgers, fries, and milkshakes, served in a fun, musical environment. Kids will love the live performances, and parents can enjoy the nostalgic vibe.

Alice's Tea Cup

Alice's Tea Cup is a whimsical tea shop that brings the world of "Alice in Wonderland" to life. It's an ideal spot for a special treat with the kids, offering a menu of teas, scones, sandwiches, and desserts that appeal to all ages.

Address

102 West 73rd Street, Manhattan (one of several locations).

How to Get There

Accessible via the B and C trains to 72nd Street or the 1, 2, and 3 trains to 72nd Street.

Opening Hours

Open daily from 11:00 AM to 6:00 PM.

Budget

Afternoon tea service ranges from $20-$40 per person.

Expect a cosy, fairy-tale setting with a menu that includes kid-friendly options like grilled cheese and cookies. Children can dress up in fairy wings and enjoy a magical tea party.

Brooklyn Farmacy & Soda Fountain

Brooklyn Farmacy & Soda Fountain is a retro-style soda shop located in a restored 1920s pharmacy. It's known for its ice cream sundaes, floats, and other nostalgic treats that delight both kids and adults.

Address

513 Henry Street, Brooklyn.

How to Get There

Accessible via the F, G trains to Carroll Street.

Opening Hours

Open Monday through Friday from 11:00 AM to 10:00 PM, weekends from 9:00 AM to 10:00 PM.

Budget

Ice cream treats range from $5-$15.

Expect a charming, old-fashioned atmosphere with counter seating and vintage decor. The menu features classic ice cream sundaes, milkshakes, and savoury items like grilled cheese.

Serendipity 3

Serendipity 3 is a famous dessert restaurant known for its extravagant sundaes and frozen hot chocolate. It's a whimsical spot perfect for a special family outing, with a menu that's sure to satisfy any sweet tooth.

Address

225 East 60th Street, Manhattan.

How to Get There

Accessible via the N, Q, R, 4, 5, 6 trains to 59th Street-Lexington Avenue.

Opening Hours

Open daily from 11:30 AM to 11:00 PM.

Budget

Desserts range from $15-$30.

Expect a quirky, eclectic setting with a menu focused on indulgent desserts and classic American fare. The frozen hot chocolate is a must-try, and the whimsical decor adds to the fun.

These child-friendly restaurants and cafés in New York City offer not only delicious food but also unique experiences that make dining out with kids a pleasure. These spots ensure that families can enjoy memorable meals together in a welcoming and entertaining environment.

Family-Friendly Broadway Shows and Entertainment

New York City is renowned for its vibrant theatre scene, and Broadway offers a selection of family-friendly shows that captivate audiences of all ages. These performances combine spectacular visuals, memorable music, and engaging stories that are perfect for kids and parents alike.

The Lion King

One of the most beloved family shows on Broadway, The Lion King brings the Disney classic to life with stunning puppetry, vibrant costumes, and unforgettable music by Elton John and Tim Rice. The show transports audiences to the African Savanna, where they follow the journey of Simba as he grows from a cub into the king of the Pride Lands.

Address

Minskoff Theatre, 200 West 45th Street, Manhattan.

How to Get There

Accessible via the 1, 2, 3, N, Q, R, W, A, C, and E trains to 42nd Street-Times Square.

Opening Hours

Showtimes vary, with matinee and evening performances.

Budget

Tickets range from $99 to $199, with discounts available through TKTS booths for same-day performances.

Expect a visually stunning production with elaborate sets and choreography that keeps both children and adults engaged. The show runs for approximately 2 hours and 30 minutes, including an intermission.

Aladdin

Aladdin is another Disney favourite that has been transformed into a Broadway spectacle. The musical follows the story of Aladdin, a young man who discovers a magical lamp and embarks on a journey that changes his life. With dazzling special effects, vibrant costumes, and songs like "A Whole New World," this show is a hit with families.

Address

New Amsterdam Theatre, 214 West 42nd Street, Manhattan.

How to Get There

Accessible via the N, Q, R, W, 1, 2, 3, A, C, and E trains to 42nd Street-Times Square.

Opening Hours

Showtimes vary, with both matinee and evening performances.

Budget

Tickets range from $79 to $169, with potential discounts through TKTS or other Broadway discount sites.

Expect a magical production with incredible sets and special effects, including the famous flying carpet scene. The show is approximately 2 hours and 30 minutes long, with an intermission.

Wicked

Wicked tells the untold story of the witches of Oz, long before Dorothy arrived. This show offers a different perspective on the classic Wizard of Oz tale, focussing on the friendship between Elphaba (the Wicked Witch of the West) and Glinda (the Good Witch). With its powerful message, stunning visuals, and memorable music by Stephen Schwartz, Wicked is a family-friendly favourite.

Address

Gershwin Theatre, 222 West 51st Street, Manhattan.

How to Get There

Accessible via the C or E trains to 50th Street or the 1 train to 50th Street.

Opening Hours

Showtimes vary, with matinee and evening performances available.

Budget

Tickets typically range from $89 to $179, with discounts sometimes available.

Expect a visually spectacular show with elaborate sets and costumes. The performance runs for about 2 hours and 45 minutes, including an intermission.

Blue Man Group

For families looking for a different kind of theatrical experience, Blue Man Group offers a unique, interactive show filled with music, comedy, and multimedia elements. The performance is highly visual and engaging, making it perfect for children and adults who enjoy something a bit out of the ordinary.

Address

Astor Place Theatre, 434 Lafayette Street, Manhattan.

How to Get There

Accessible via the 6 train to Astor Place or the N, R, W trains to 8th Street-NYU.

Opening Hours

Showtimes vary, with evening and weekend performances.

Budget

Tickets range from $59 to $129, with various discounts available.

Expect an interactive, high-energy show that features music, art, and a lot of surprises. The show is about 90 minutes long, with no intermission.

These family-friendly Broadway shows and performances provide unforgettable experiences that both kids and parents will enjoy.

Exploring New York City with kids is an adventure filled with discovery, excitement, and unforgettable experiences. The city offers endless opportunities for family fun, blending education, entertainment, and outdoor activities. With thoughtful planning, you can create memories that your children will cherish for years to come. New York City provides a rich environment for kids to learn, play, and explore in one of the world's most dynamic cities.

Chapter 8

Dining in New York City

New York City is a culinary hub, offering an incredible diversity of dining experiences that reflect its multicultural makeup. You will be guided on the best ways to experience the city's food culture, ensuring that every meal adds to the excitement of your visit.

NYC Foods

New York City is a culinary melting pot, and its iconic foods reflect the city's diverse heritage and fast-paced lifestyle. These dishes have become symbols of NYC, loved by both locals and tourists for their unique flavoursflavours and accessibility.

New York-Style Pizza

New York-style pizza is famous for its thin, foldable crust and generous toppings of cheese and tomato sauce. Originating from Italian immigrants in the early 20th century, this pizza is characterised by its large slices and simple yet flavourful ingredients. The crust is typically hand-tossed, with a light and airy texture around the edges. What sets New York-style pizza apart is its perfect balance of a crispy base and chewy interior, making it easy to fold and eat on the go.

Where to Get It

Joe's Pizza

Di Fara Pizza

Bagels with Lox and Schmear

The New York bagel is a dense, chewy bread roll with a shiny crust, often topped with seeds. It's traditionally boiled before being baked, which gives it its unique texture. The classic New York combination includes a bagel sliced in half, spread with a "schmear" of cream cheese, and topped with thinly sliced lox (cured salmon). This dish is a staple of New York's Jewish delis, reflecting the city's rich immigrant history.

Where to Get It

Russ & Daughters

Ess-a-Bagel

New York Cheesecake

New York cheesecake is rich, dense, and creamy, made primarily from cream cheese, eggs, and sugar on a GrahamGraham cracker crust. Unlike other varieties, New York cheesecake is known for its dense texture, achieved by adding extra egg yolks to the batter. It's typically served plain or with a topping of fresh fruit or a drizzle of chocolate.

Where to Get It

Junior's

Eileen's Special Cheesecake

Hot Dogs

The New York hot dog is a simple yet iconic street food, usually served with mustard and sauerkraut or onions. The hot dog is a quick and satisfying snack, reflecting the city's fast-paced lifestyle. Nathan's Famous, originating from Coney Island, helped popularisepopularise this classic, and today hot dog carts can be found on almost every corner of the city.

Where to Get It

Nathan's Famous

Gray's Papaya

New York Deli Sandwiches

New York delis are renowned for their oversized sandwiches, particularly the pastrami on rye. This sandwich features tender, spiced pastrami piled high on rye bread, often served with mustard and a pickle on the side. The quality of the pastrami, which is cured and smoked, is what makes this sandwich truly special.

Where to Get It

Katz's Delicatessen

2nd Ave Deli

These New York foods not only satisfy your taste buds but also offer a taste of the city's cultural and culinary history.

These dishes are an essential part of the New York City experience.

Fine Dining and Michelin-Star Restaurants

New York City is home to some of the finest dining experiences in the world, with several Michelin-starred restaurants offering exquisite cuisine, impeccable service, and an unforgettable atmosphere. These establishments are renowned not just for their food but for the complete dining experience they provide, making them a must-visit for people seeking a taste of culinary excellence.

Eleven Madison Park

Eleven Madison Park is one of the most celebrated restaurants in the city, known for its innovative approach to contemporary American cuisine. The restaurant boasts three Michelin stars and has consistently ranked among the best in the world. With a focus on plant-based dishes, Eleven Madison Park offers a tasting menu that highlights seasonal and local ingredients, presented with artistic flair.

Scan the QR code to visit Eleven Madison Park's website

Address

11 Madison Avenue, Manhattan.

How to Get There

Accessible via the 6, N, andN, and R trains to 23rd Street.

Opening Hours

Dinner service from Tuesday to Saturday, with seating from 5:00 PM.

Budget

Tasting menu priced at around $335 per person, excluding beverages and service charges.

The restaurant's attention to detail extends to the wine pairings, which are carefully curated to complement the menu.

Expect to see an elegant dining room with attentive service, where every dish is a masterpiece. The restaurant caters to a sophisticated clientele, and the dress code is formal. Expect a dining experience that lasts several hours, with each course carefully explained by the staff.

Le Bernardin

Le Bernardin is a temple of seafood, earning three Michelin stars and international acclaim for its pristine, artfully prepared dishes. Helmed by Chef Eric Ripert, Le Bernardin focuses on seafood in its purest form, letting the quality of the ingredients shine through in every dish. The restaurant is a favourite among both locals and tourists for special occasions.

Scan the QR code to visit Le Bernardin's website

Address

155 West 51st Street, Manhattan.

How to Get There

Accessible via the B, D, and E trains to 7th Avenue.

Opening Hours

Lunch from Tuesday to Friday, 12:00 PM to 2:30 PM; dinner from Monday to Saturday, 5:15 PM to 10:30 PM.

Budget

Tasting menus range from $198 to $275 per person, with additional wine pairings available.

The wine list is extensive, with sommelier-guided pairings that enhance the flavours of each course.

Expect a serene, sophisticated ambiance with a focus on impeccable service. The menu offers both prix-fixe and tasting options, with a focus on delicate, perfectly executed seafood dishes. The dress code is business attire, and the clientele includes both business professionals and discerning food lovers.

Per Se

Per Se, a three-Michelin-starred restaurant by Chef Thomas Keller, offers a dining experience that is both luxurious and deeply personal. The restaurant's menu features French and American influences, with a focus on precision and refinement. Located in the Time Warner Centre, Per Se provides stunning views of Central Park, adding to the overall experience.

Scan the QR code to visit Per Se's website

Address

10 Columbus Circle, Manhattan.

How to Get There

Accessible via the A, C, B, D, and 1 trains to 59th Street-Columbus Circle.

Opening Hours

Dinner service daily from 5:30 PM to 9:30 PM; lunch on weekends from 11:30 AM to 1:00 PM.

Budget

Tasting menu priced at around $355 per person, excluding beverages and service charges.

Expect a tranquil, sophisticated environment with a focus on extraordinary service. The menu changes daily, offering a nine-course tasting experience that reflects the finest seasonal ingredients. The restaurant enforces a strict dress code (jackets required), and the experience is meant to be leisurely, with the meal lasting several hours.

Per Se also offers a vegetable tasting menu, and its extensive wine list features rare and exclusive selections.

What to Expect at Michelin-Starred Restaurants in NYC

Dining at a Michelin-starred restaurant in New York City is not just about the food, it's about the entire experience. These restaurants are known for their attention to detail, from the décor and ambiance to the presentation of each dish. Service is typically impeccable, with knowledgeable staff who guide you through the menu and wine list, ensuring that your meal is perfectly tailored to your tastes.

Reservations are often required well in advance, particularly for dinner services at these renowned establishments. The dining experience is usually unhurried, with multiple courses and carefully timed service that allows you to savour each dish. Dress codes are strictly enforced, reflecting the formal and upscale nature of these venues.

These Michelin-starred restaurants offer some of the finest cuisine in the world, set against the backdrop of one of the most dynamic cities.

Budget-Friendly Restaurants

New York City is known for its diverse culinary scene, and there are plenty of budget-friendly options that deliver big on flavour without breaking the bank. These restaurants are beloved by both locals and tourists for their affordability and quality, offering a true taste of NYC without the hefty price tag.

Joe's Pizza

Joe's Pizza is a quintessential New York slice joint that has been serving up classic, no-frills pizza since 1975. It's an iconic spot for grabbing a quick, delicious slice, whether you're on the go or want to sit and people-watch.

Scan the QR code to visit Joe's Pizza's website

Address

7 Carmine Street, Manhattan (Original Location).

How to Get There

Accessible via the A, B, C, D, E, F, and M trains to West 4th Street-Washington Square.

Opening Hours

Open daily from 10:00 AM to 4:00 AM.

Budget

$3 per slice, $20 for a whole pie.

You'll see thin, foldable slices with a crispy crust and the perfect balance of sauce and cheese. The atmosphere is casual, with quick service ideal for those on the move.

Mamouns Falafel

Scan the QR code to visit Mamouns Falafel's Pizza's website

Mamouns Falafel is one of the city's oldest falafel joints, offering authentic Middle Eastern cuisine at incredibly affordable prices. This Greenwich Village institution is famous for its falafel sandwiches, shawarma, and hummus.

Address

119 MacDougal Street, Manhattan.

How to Get There

Accessible via the A, B, C, D, E, F, and M trains to West 4th Street-Washington Square.

Opening Hours

Open daily from 11:00 a.m. to 5:00 a.m.

Budget

Sandwiches start at $4, platters at $7.

Expect a quick-service counter with limited seating, offering flavourful, fresh food perfect for a budget-friendly meal. Expect a lively, bustling atmosphere, especially late at night.

Katz's Delicatessen

Katz's Delicatessen is a historic New York deli famous for its pastrami sandwiches. While slightly higher in price, the portions are massive, making it a great value for those wanting to experience an iconic NYC deli without splurging too much.

Address

205 East Houston Street, Manhattan.

How to Get There

Accessible via the F train to 2nd Avenue.

Opening Hours

Open Monday to Wednesday from 8:00 AM to 10:45 PM, Thursday to Sunday from 8:00 AM to 2:45 AM.

Budget

Sandwiches around $25, but easily shareable.

Expect an authentic New York deli experience with an old-school vibe. The food is rich and filling, perfect for sharing or taking some home.

What to Expect at Budget-Friendly Restaurants in NYC

These budget-friendly spots are designed for quick service and high turnover, catering to both locals and tourists who want a delicious meal without spending too much. The atmosphere in these establishments is typically casual and bustling, often with counter service and limited seating. Despite the lower prices, these restaurants don't compromise on quality, offering some of the best and most authentic tastes of New York City.

These budget-friendly restaurants ensure you can experience the diverse flavours of New York City without stretching your wallet.

Street Food and Food Trucks

New York City is a paradise for street food lovers, offering a diverse array of flavours from around the world. Street food and food trucks are a staple of the city, serving everything from classic New York hot dogs to gourmet international cuisine. These mobile kitchens provide quick, delicious meals that are beloved by both locals and tourists.

The Halal Guys

The Halal Guys started as a simple food cart and has grown into an iconic brand known for its generous portions of gyro meat, chicken, and falafel, served with rice, pita, and their famous white and hot sauces. It's a must-try for anyone looking to experience NYC street food at its best.

Address

53rd Street & 6th Avenue, Manhattan.

How to Get There

Accessible via the B, D, and E trains to 7th Avenue.

Opening Hours

Open daily from 10:00 AM to 4:00 AM.

Budget

$8-$10 per platter.

Expect long lines, especially during lunch and late-night hours, but the wait is worth it. The food is flavourful, filling, and perfect for a quick, satisfying meal.

Korilla BBQ

Korilla BBQ is a popular food truck that blends Korean BBQ flavours with a modern twist. Known for their build-your-own bowls, wraps, and burritos, Korilla offers a unique fusion of spicy, tangy, and savoury flavours, making it a hit with foodies on the go.

Address

Locations vary; check their social media or website for the daily schedule.

How to Get There

Various locations around Manhattan, often near Midtown or Downtown.

Opening Hours

Typically open for lunch from 11:00 AM to 3:00 PM, but hours can vary.

Budget

$10-$15 per meal.

They offer fresh, made-to-order meals with bold flavors. The truck offers customisable options, allowing you to choose your protein, rice, and toppings.

NY Dosas

NY Dosas is a beloved vegan food cart located in Washington Square Park, serving up South Indian dosas (savoury crepes) filled with spiced potatoes, lentils, and other vegetarian delights. This cart has garnered a loyal following for its delicious and affordable meals.

Address

Washington Square Park, Manhattan.

How to Get There

Accessible via the A, B, C, D, E, F, and M trains to West 4th Street-Washington Square.

Opening Hours

Typically open from 11:00 AM to 3:00 PM, but the cart may close early if they sell out.

Budget

$6-$9 per meal.

Expect a friendly vendor, fresh ingredients, and a unique take on vegan street food. Lines can be long, but the food is worth the wait, especially for those seeking a healthy, flavourful option.

Uncle Gussy's

Uncle Gussy's is a well-loved food truck serving authentic Greek cuisine, including gyros, souvlaki, and other Mediterranean delights. Located in Midtown, it's a popular spot for a quick, tasty lunch.

Address

51st Street & Park Avenue, Manhattan.

How to Get There

Accessible via the 6, E, and M trains to 51st Street-Lexington Avenue.

Opening Hours

Open Monday to Friday from 11:00 AM to 3:00 PM.

Budget

$8-$12 per meal.

Expect generous portions of grilled meats, fresh salads, and homemade tzatziki sauce. The food is fresh, flavourful, and served quickly, making it a perfect stop for a satisfying meal on the go.

What to Expect from NYC Street Food and Food Trucks

Street food and food trucks in New York City are all about convenience, flavour, and variety. The atmosphere is casual, with most food being served to-go, allowing you to enjoy your meal in one of the city's many parks or on a bench nearby. While lines can be long, especially at popular spots, the service is generally fast and efficient.

Prices are typically affordable, making it easy to sample a variety of dishes without overspending. These food vendors cater to a wide audience, from busy office workers to tourists looking for a quick and tasty bite.

NYC's street food and food trucks offer a diverse range of options that showcase the city's rich culinary landscape.

Vegetarian and Vegan Dining Options

New York City is a haven for vegetarian and vegan diners, offering a wide range of plant-based restaurants that cater to both locals and tourists. From creative fine dining to comforting fast-casual spots, these eateries are known for their innovative use of ingredients and commitment to sustainable, ethical food practices.

Superiority Burger

Superiority Burger is a small, popular eatery in the East Village, known for its inventive vegetarian and vegan fare. Their signature dish, the Superiority Burger, is a must-try—a savoury veggie burger that's garnered a cult following. The menu is seasonal, featuring a rotating selection of salads, sides, and desserts that highlight fresh, local produce.

Address

119 Avenue A, Manhattan.

How to Get There

Accessible via the L train to 1st Avenue or the F train to 2nd Avenue.

Opening Hours

Open Monday to Saturday from 12:00 PM to 10:00 PM; closed on Sundays.

Budget

$10-$15 per meal.

Expect a cosy, no-frills spot with limited seating, offering a relaxed atmosphere. The food is served quickly, and the casual vibe makes it perfect for a quick lunch or dinner.

Dirt Candy

Dirt Candy is a celebrated vegetarian fine dining restaurant that takes plant-based cuisine to a new level. Chef Amanda Cohen's inventive dishes are as visually stunning as they are delicious, with a focus on vegetables as the star of every plate. The menu changes seasonally and features creative takes on classic dishes.

Scan the QR code to visit Dirt Candy's website

Address

86 Allen Street, Manhattan.

How to Get There

Accessible via the F, M, J, Z trains to Delancey Street-Essex Street.

Opening Hours

Open Tuesday to Saturday from 5:30 PM to 10:30 PM; closed Sunday and Monday.

Budget

Tasting menu priced at around $95 per person.

Expect a sleek, modern dining room with an open kitchen, allowing guests to watch their meals being prepared. The experience is refined and leisurely, perfect for a special occasion or an elegant night out.

Peacefood Cafe

Peacefood Cafe is a beloved vegan café offering a wide variety of plant-based dishes, from hearty sandwiches and soups to delicious desserts. With a focus on wholesome ingredients and sustainability, Peacefood Cafe is popular among both vegans and non-vegans alike.

Scan the QR code to visit Peacefood Cafe's website

Address

460 Amsterdam Avenue, Manhattan (Upper West Side location).

How to Get There

Accessible via the 1, 2, and 3 trains to 72nd Street or the B and C trains to 72nd Street.

Opening Hours

Open daily from 11:00 AM to 10:00 PM.

Budget

$10-$20 per meal.

Expect a cosy, welcoming space with a laid-back vibe. The menu includes a wide range of options, from light bites to full meals, all made with fresh, organic ingredients.

What to Expect at Vegetarian and Vegan Restaurants in NYC

New York City's vegetarian and vegan restaurants are known for their creativity, quality, and commitment to sustainability. These establishments cater to a diverse clientele, from lifelong vegans to those simply looking to try something new. The atmosphere in these restaurants ranges from casual and friendly to refined and elegant, ensuring there's something for every occasion.

Meals are typically made with fresh, local, and organic ingredients, with menus that change seasonally to reflect the best produce available. Whether you're indulging in a gourmet tasting menu or grabbing a quick plant-based burger, NYC's vegetarian and vegan dining scene offers something for everyone.

Ethnic Cuisine

New York City is a melting pot of cultures, and its diverse population has brought an incredible variety of global flavours to the city's dining scene. From authentic Italian pasta to spicy Indian curries, NYC offers a culinary journey around the world, right within its boroughs. These ethnic restaurants are beloved, offering a taste of home for immigrants and an adventure for food lovers.

Di Fara Pizza

Scan the QR code to visit Di Fara Pizza's website

For an authentic taste of Italian-American cuisine, head to Di Fara Pizza in Brooklyn. Established in 1965 by Domenico DeMarco, Di Fara has earned a legendary status for its handcrafted pizzas, made with imported Italian ingredients and baked to perfection in a classic oven. Each pizza is made to order, ensuring a fresh and flavourful experience.

Address

1424 Avenue J, Brooklyn.

How to Get There

Accessible via the Q train to Avenue J.

Opening Hours

Open Wednesday to Sunday from 12:00 PM to 8:00 PM.

Budget

Pizzas start at $30 for a whole pie, reflecting the quality and craftsmanship.

Expect a small, unassuming pizzeria with a no-frills atmosphere. Expect to wait for your pizza, as each one is made individually, but the delicious, crispy crust and perfectly balanced flavours make it worth the wait.

The Bao

The Bao is a popular spot in the East Village, specialising in Chinese cuisine, particularly known for its soup dumplings (xiao long bao). These delicate dumplings are filled with a rich, savoury broth and tender pork, offering an authentic taste of Shanghai street food. The Bao also serves a variety of other traditional Chinese dishes.

Scan the QR code to visit The Bao's website

Address

13 St. Marks Place, Manhattan.

How to Get There

Accessible via the 6 train to Astor Place or the L train to 1st Avenue.

Opening Hours

Open daily from 11:30 AM to 10:00 PM.

Budget

Dishes range from $10-$20, with affordable options for sharing.

Expect a lively atmosphere with quick service and a focus on quality. The restaurant is often busy, but the turnover is fast, making it a great spot for a casual lunch or dinner.

La Esquina

La Esquina offers a unique blend of traditional and modern Mexican cuisine, serving everything from street tacos to more sophisticated dishes. The restaurant is known for its authentic flavours and cool, underground vibe. La Esquina operates as a taqueria during the day, but by night, it transforms into a hidden speakeasy-style dining experience.

Address

114 Kenmare Street, Manhattan.

How to Get There

Accessible via the 6 train to Spring Street.

Opening Hours

The taqueria is open daily from 8:00 AM to 11:00 PM, while the brasserie opens for dinner service from 6:00 PM to 2:00 AM.

Budget

Tacos start at $5 each, with main courses in the brasserie ranging from $20-$40.

Expect a trendy atmosphere with delicious, authentic Mexican food. The underground brasserie is a hidden gem, offering a more intimate dining experience.

What to Expect at Ethnic Restaurants in NYC

New York City's ethnic restaurants are celebrated for their authenticity, often run by immigrants who bring their culinary traditions to the city. These establishments range from casual, hole-in-the-wall eateries to more upscale dining experiences, but all share a commitment to preserving the flavours and techniques of their native cuisines.

The atmosphere in these restaurants can vary widely. Service is typically friendly and efficient, with many places offering dishes meant for sharing. The prices can range from very affordable to moderately expensive, depending on the ingredients and preparation involved.

NYC's ethnic restaurants offer a world of flavours to explore, each providing a unique taste of the diverse cultures that make up the fabric of the city.

Dining in New York City is an essential part of experiencing the city's vibrant culture. As you explore NYC's culinary landscape, you'll find that the flavours and traditions of its food scene add a rich layer to your visit, making every bite a memorable part of your journey through the city.

CHAPTER 9

Nightlife and Entertainment

New York City offers a dynamic and diverse nightlife scene that caters to every taste. The city offers endless possibilities for entertainment.

Nightclubs and Lounges

New York City's nightlife is legendary, offering trendy clubs and sophisticated lounges that cater to every taste.

The Box

The Box is not just a nightclub; it's an experience. Known for its risqué performances and theatrical shows, The Box offers a blend of nightlife and entertainment that's truly unique. The venue combines a cabaret-style theatre with a nightclub, creating an eclectic and immersive experience.

Scan the QR code to visit The Box's website

Location

189 Chrystie Street, Manhattan.

How to Get There

Accessible via the F train to 2nd Avenue or the J, Z trains to Bowery.

Budget

Entry fees vary depending on the night, but expect to pay around $40-$50. Shows and bottle service can significantly increase the cost.

Expect a provocative and dramatic atmosphere with live performances that range from burlesque to avant-garde. The crowd is typically trendy and artsy, with a dress code that leans towards the extravagant.

Le Bain

Le Bain is a rooftop nightclub and lounge located atop The Standard Hotel in the Meatpacking District. The venue offers stunning views of the Hudson River and the Manhattan skyline, making it a popular spot for both tourists and locals. With a dance floor, a plunge pool, and an outdoor terrace, Le Bain provides a dynamic nightlife experience.

Location

848 Washington Street, Manhattan.

How to Get There

Accessible via the A, C, E, and L trains to 14th Street or the 1, 2, and 3 trains to 14th Street.

Budget

Entry is often free but can vary depending on events. Drinks are on the pricier side, with cocktails averaging $15-$20.

Expect a mix of laid-back lounging and energetic dancing, with different vibes depending on the night. The rooftop offers a great place to relax, while the dance floor heats up later in the evening. Expect a diverse crowd and a casual-chic dress code.

PHD Lounge at Dream Downtown

PHD Lounge, located on the rooftop of the Dream Downtown hotel, is a chic and glamorous spot offering panoramic views of the Manhattan skyline. The lounge is known for its stylish crowd, inventive cocktails, and upscale ambiance.

Location

355 West 16th Street, Manhattan.

How to Get There

Accessible via the A, C, E, and L trains to 14th Street or the 1, 2, and 3 trains to 18th Street.

Budget

Cocktails start at around $18, with entry fees varying based on the night and event.

Expect to see a good atmosphere with top-notch service and a well-dressed crowd. The venue is perfect for those looking to enjoy a night out in style, with plush seating and ambient lighting adding to the luxurious vibe.

What to Expect at NYC Nightclubs and Lounges

NYC's nightclubs and lounges offer a variety of experiences, from high-energy dance floors to intimate settings for a quiet drink. Most venues enforce a dress code, so plan to dress smartly. Entry fees can vary widely, and popular spots often have long lines, so it's advisable to arrive early or consider table reservations. The crowd tends to be a mix of locals and tourists, with the atmosphere ranging from casual to upscale depending on the location. Whether you're in the mood for dancing or just want to enjoy a cocktail with a view, New York City's nightlife has something to offer everyone.

Live Music Venues and Jazz Clubs

New York City has a rich tradition of live music, particularly in its legendary jazz clubs and vibrant music venues. These spots offer an authentic slice of the city's musical culture. From historic clubs that have hosted jazz legends to intimate spaces where you can catch up-and-coming bands, the city's live music scene is both diverse and dynamic.

The Blue Note

The Blue Note is one of NYC's most famous jazz clubs, known for hosting some of the biggest names in jazz history, from Miles Davis to Herbie Hancock. Located in Greenwich Village, it offers an intimate setting where jazz lovers can enjoy world-class performances up close.

Scan the QR code to visit The Blue Note's website

Location

131 West 3rd Street, Manhattan.

How to Get There

Accessible via the A, B, C, D, E, F, and M trains to West 4th Street-Washington Square.

Budget

Tickets generally range from $30 to $85, depending on the performer and seating.

Expect a cosy, atmospheric venue with top-notch acoustics and a diverse lineup of jazz artists. Reservations are recommended, especially for weekend shows. The Blue Note also offers a dinner menu, so you can enjoy a meal while taking in the music.

Village Vanguard

The Village Vanguard is another iconic jazz club, with a history dating back to 1935. This legendary spot has seen performances from virtually every major jazz artist over the decades and continues to be a cornerstone of the jazz scene in NYC. The club's intimate, basement setting creates an unparalleled experience for jazz enthusiasts.

Scan the QR code to visit Village Vanguard's website

Location

178 7th Avenue South, Manhattan.

How to Get There

Accessible via the 1, 2, and 3 trains to 14th Street.

Budget

Tickets are typically $30 for most performances, with a one-drink minimum per set.

Expect an intimate venue where the focus is entirely on the music. The Village Vanguard is known for its excellent acoustics and serious jazz-loving crowd. Shows often sell out, so it's advisable to book in advance.

Bowery Ballroom

For those looking to explore NYC's indie and rock scene, Bowery Ballroom is a must-visit. Located in the Lower East Side, this venue is known for its exceptional sound quality and diverse lineup, featuring everything from indie rock bands to emerging artists.

Location

6 Delancey Street, Manhattan.

How to Get There

Accessible via the J, Z trains to Bowery or the F train to 2nd Avenue.

Budget

Ticket prices vary widely depending on the artist, typically ranging from $20 to $50.

Expect a classic New York music venue with a standing-room-only main floor and a balcony for seated viewing. The intimate space and excellent acoustics make it a favourite among both artists and fans. The venue also features a bar with reasonably priced drinks.

Smalls Jazz Club

Smalls Jazz Club is a cosy, underground venue in Greenwich Village, known for its intimate atmosphere and late-night jam sessions. It's a great spot to catch both established and up-and-coming jazz musicians in a setting that feels authentically New York.

Location

183 West 10th Street, Manhattan.

How to Get There

Accessible via the 1 train to Christopher Street-Sheridan Square or the A, C, E, B, D, F, and M trains to West 4th Street-Washington Square.

Budget

Cover charges typically range from $20 to $30, with no minimum drink purchase.

Expect a small, laid-back venue where the focus is purely on the music. Smalls is known for its friendly, inclusive vibe and for featuring some of the best jazz talent in the city.

What to Expect at NYC Live Music Venues and Jazz Clubs

Live music venues and jazz clubs in New York City each have their own unique atmosphere, but they all share a deep respect for the music. You can expect top-tier performances and a crowd that's there to appreciate the talent.

Most venues offer drinks, and some also serve food, though it's the music that's the main draw. Tickets can vary in price, and it's often best to buy them in advance, especially for popular shows. Arrive early to get a good spot, particularly in venues with limited seating.

New York City's live music scene is a rich part of its cultural fabric, offering something for every music lover. Whether you're in the mood for a classic jazz performance or want to discover the next big thing in indie rock, the city's venues provide unforgettable experiences for locals and tourists alike.

Comedy Clubs and Themed Bars

New York City's nightlife isn't just about nightclubs and live music; it also boasts some of the best comedy clubs and themed bars in the world. These venues offer unique experiences where you can enjoy a laugh or immerse yourself in a creatively themed environment.

Comedy Cellar

Comedy Cellar is perhaps the most famous comedy club in New York City, known for its intimate setting and a lineup that regularly features top comedians, including household names like Chris Rock and Amy Schumer. It's the perfect place to catch a live stand-up show with an authentic New York vibe.

Scan the QR code to visit **Comedy Cellar**'*s website*

Location

117 MacDougal Street, Manhattan.

How to Get There

Accessible via the A, B, C, D, E, F, and M trains to West 4th Street-Washington Square.

Budget

Tickets typically range from $20 to $30, with a two-drink minimum.

Expect to see a packed, cosy venue with shows that often sell out, so booking in advance is recommended. The atmosphere is lively, and the lineup is consistently top-notch. You might even catch a surprise set from a well-known comedian.

The Stand

The Stand is another top comedy club in NYC, offering a mix of stand-up comedy and a full-service restaurant. Located in the Gramercy area, The Stand features both up-and-coming and well-established comedians, making it a great spot for a night of laughs and good food.

Location

116 East 16th Street, Manhattan.

How to Get There

Accessible via the 4, 5, 6, L, N, Q, R, W trains to 14th Street-Union Square.

Budget

Tickets range from $15 to $40, depending on the performer, with a two-drink minimum.

Expect to see a modern, comfortable venue with a solid lineup of comedians. The Stand is also known for its excellent food, so consider having dinner before or during the show.

The Cauldron NYC

For a unique bar experience, The Cauldron NYC is a magical themed bar where patrons can create their own potions (cocktails) using a mix of science and fantasy. The bar offers an immersive experience inspired by magic and fantasy literature, complete with interactive elements and themed decor.

Scan the QR code to visit The Cauldron NYC's website

Location

127 W 26th St, New York.

How to Get There

Accessible via the 1, 2, 3, 4, 5, R, W trains to Wall Street.

Budget

The potion-making experience costs around $45 per person.

Expect a whimsical atmosphere with themed cocktails and a focus on interactive fun. The experience is highly engaging, making it a great spot for groups or a unique date night.

Please Don't Tell (PDT)

Please Don't Tell is a hidden speakeasy located behind a hot dog shop in the East Village. This intimate bar is known for its creative cocktails and secretive vibe, offering a throwback to Prohibition-era speakeasies. The entrance is through a phone booth inside Crif Dogs, where you dial a number to gain entry.

Location

113 St. Marks Place, Manhattan.

How to Get There

Accessible via the L train to 1st Avenue.

Budget

Cocktails range from $15 to $20.

Expect an intimate, dimly lit space with a focus on craft cocktails. The bar has a small, exclusive feel, making reservations essential. Expect expertly mixed drinks in a cosy, secretive environment.

What to Expect at Comedy Clubs and Themed Bars in NYC

New York City's comedy clubs and themed bars offer a range of experiences, like laugh-out-loud stand-up shows and immersive, themed environments. Comedy clubs like Comedy Cellar and The Stand are known for attracting top talent, so you're guaranteed a great show, often at an affordable price. Themed bars like The Cauldron and PDT provide unique, interactive experiences that go beyond just having a drink.

Booking in advance is often recommended, especially for popular comedy shows or speakeasies with limited seating. Dress codes vary depending on the venue, but most places maintain a casual yet stylish atmosphere.

Late-Night Eateries

New York City is the city that never sleeps, and its food scene is no different. Late-night eateries across the city offer a variety of options for night owls craving a bite after hours, ranging from classic diners to trendy spots serving everything from burgers to international delicacies.

Katz's Delicatessen

Katz's Delicatessen is an iconic New York institution that has been serving up its famous pastrami sandwiches since 1888. Open late into the night, it's the perfect spot for those craving a hearty meal after a night out. The no-frills deli atmosphere adds to its charm, making it a must-visit for both locals and tourists.

Veselka

Veselka is a 24-hour Ukrainian diner in the East Village, known for its comforting Eastern European dishes. Whether you're in the mood for pierogi, borscht, or hearty breakfast fare, Veselka offers a warm and welcoming atmosphere, no matter the hour.

Location

144 2nd Avenue, Manhattan.

How to Get There

Accessible via the L train to 1st Avenue or the 6 train to Astor Place.

Budget

Dishes range from $10 to $20, with generous portions.

Expect a cosy, diner-style setting with friendly service. Veselka is a favourite among locals for both its food and its history, making it a great spot for a late-night meal.

Bubby's

Bubby's, located in Tribeca, is a classic American eatery known for its comfort food and pies. Open late on weekends, it's a popular spot for a late-night brunch or dinner. The atmosphere is laid-back, and the menu features everything from burgers to pancakes.

Location

120 Hudson Street, Manhattan.

How to Get There

Accessible via the 1, 2, 3, A, C, and E trains to Canal Street.

Budget

Entrees typically range from $15 to $25.

Expect a relaxed, family-friendly environment with a focus on quality, homemade dishes. The restaurant is known for its pies, so be sure to save room for dessert.

Joe's Pizza

Joe's Pizza is a legendary slice joint in Greenwich Village, serving up classic New York-style pizza since 1975. Open until the early hours, Joe's is the go-to spot for a quick, delicious slice after a night out. The no-frills pizzeria offers a true taste of New York.

What to Expect at NYC's Late-Night Eateries

New York's late-night eateries are designed to cater to the city's nocturnal crowd, offering quick, satisfying meals long after other places have closed. Expect a diverse range of food options, like comfort food and international cuisine, served in relaxed, often bustling environments. These spots offer something for every palate, with the added bonus of being open when most other places aren't.

New York City's entertainment and nightlife scene is truly unparalleled, offering a wide array of experiences that cater to every interest and mood. The energy and diversity of NYC's nightlife make it an essential part of the city's identity, ensuring that your evenings are as memorable as your days.

CHAPTER 10

Seasonal Events and Festivals

New York City's seasons bring their own unique events and festivals. These gatherings showcase the city's diverse culture, creativity, and community spirit, offering something special no matter when you visit.

Spring Festivals and Events

Spring in New York City brings a vibrant array of festivals and events that celebrate the season's renewal and the city's diverse culture. As the weather warms, the city comes alive with outdoor activities, parades, and celebrations that attract both locals and tourists.

Macy's Flower Show

Held annually at Macy's Herald Square, the Macy's Flower Show is a two-week-long event that transforms the department store into a floral wonderland. The show typically starts at the end of March and runs through early April, showcasing elaborate flower displays and themed gardens.

Date

Late March to early April.

Dress Code

Casual, comfortable shoes are recommended for walking through the exhibits.

Time

The store is open during regular business hours, usually from 10:00 AM to 9:00 PM.

Expect to see stunning floral displays, free to the public. Expect crowds, especially on weekends. Bring a camera to capture the beautiful arrangements.

Tribeca Film Festival

The Tribeca Film Festival, founded by Robert De Niro in 2002, celebrates film, music, and culture with screenings, panels, and performances throughout Lower Manhattan. The festival typically runs for two weeks in April, attracting filmmakers, celebrities, and film enthusiasts from around the world.

Date

Early June

Dress Code

Smart casual; dress comfortably for walking and standing at various venues.

Time

Screenings and events take place throughout the day and evening.

Expect a mix of film premieres, documentaries, short films, and interactive experiences. Tickets should be purchased in advance, and bringing along a light jacket is advisable as evenings can still be cool.

Sakura Matsuri Cherry Blossom Festival

Held at the Brooklyn Botanic Garden, the Sakura Matsuri Cherry Blossom Festival is a celebration of Japanese culture and the blooming cherry blossoms. The two-day event usually takes place at the end of April, offering performances, workshops, and traditional Japanese arts.

Date

Late April.

Dress Code

Casual; many attendees dress in Japanese attire, including kimonos and cosplay.

Time

The event runs from 10:00 AM to 6:00 PM each day.

You'll see beautiful cherry blossoms, cultural performances, tea ceremonies, and art exhibits. Bring a picnic blanket and enjoy the day under the cherry trees.

Tickets can be purchased online, and early arrival is recommended to avoid crowds.

Easter Parade and Bonnet Festival

The Easter Parade and Bonnet Festival is a quirky and colourful event that takes place on Easter Sunday along Fifth Avenue. Participants and spectators don extravagant hats and costumes, turning the parade into a lively fashion show.

Date

Easter Sunday (date varies each year).

Dress Code

Festive attire; wear your most creative hat or bonnet.

Time

The parade typically runs from 10:00 AM to 4:00 PM.

Expect to see a joyful and informal parade with participants of all ages. No tickets are required, and the event is free to attend. Bring along a camera to capture the whimsical hats and outfits.

What to Bring and Additional Tips

For spring events in New York City, it's wise to bring along a light jacket or sweater, as temperatures can vary throughout the day. Comfortable shoes are essential for walking, especially at events with large crowds or outdoor venues. It's also a good idea to bring a camera or smartphone for photos, as many of these events offer beautiful and unique sights. Finally, plan to arrive early to secure good spots, especially for popular events like parades and festivals.

Summer in the City

Summer in New York City is a season of vibrant outdoor activities, with the city coming alive through concerts, festivals, and various cultural events. The long days and warm nights create the perfect backdrop for enjoying the best of what the city has to offer under the open sky.

Central Park SummerStage

Central Park SummerStage is one of the city's most beloved summer traditions, offering free concerts and performances in the heart of Central Park. The event runs from June through August and features a diverse lineup of artists across genres, including rock, jazz, hip-hop, and classical music.

Date

June through August.

Dress Code

Casual and comfortable; bring a light jacket for cooler evenings.

Time

Concerts typically start in the late afternoon or early evening.

Expect a lively, diverse crowd enjoying live music in a beautiful outdoor setting. Seating is on the lawn, so bring a blanket or low chair, along with snacks and water. Arrive early to secure a good spot, as popular shows can fill up quickly.

Shakespeare in the Park

Shakespeare in the Park is an annual summer event held at the Delacorte Theatre in Central Park, offering free performances of Shakespeare's plays. The event is a cherished New York tradition, attracting both locals and visitors eager to enjoy theatre under the stars.

Date

Typically runs from June through August.

Dress Code

Casual; be prepared for the weather as performances continue, rain or shine.

Time

Evening performances usually start at 8:00 PM.

You'll see high-quality, free theatre in a beautiful outdoor venue. Tickets are free but must be obtained through a lottery or by waiting in line at the park. Bring a blanket or cushion for added comfort, and consider packing a picnic to enjoy before the show.

Bryant Park Movie Nights

Bryant Park Movie Nights offer free outdoor movie screenings on the lawn of Bryant Park, providing a laid-back way to enjoy classic films in the heart of Manhattan. The event typically runs from June through August, with movies shown on Monday evenings.

Date

June through August.

Dress Code

Casual; bring layers for cooler evenings.

Time

Movies usually start at sunset, around 8:00 PM.

Expect a relaxed atmosphere with locals and tourists enjoying movies on the grass. Bring a blanket, snacks, and drinks to create your own picnic. Arrive early to find a good spot, as the lawn can fill up quickly.

Pride Parade and PrideFest

The NYC Pride Parade and PrideFest are major events that celebrate LGBTQ+ pride and equality. The parade is one of the largest in the world and takes place in late June, coinciding with the anniversary of the Stonewall Riots. The event features colourful floats, performances, and a vibrant atmosphere of celebration.

Date

Late June, typically the last Sunday of the month.

Dress Code

Festive and colourful; many attendees wear rainbow-themed outfits.

Time

The parade starts in the late morning and continues into the afternoon.

Expect a lively, inclusive atmosphere with a mix of parade floats, performers, and spectators. PrideFest, a street fair, usually follows the parade, offering food, merchandise, and live entertainment. Bring sunscreen, water, and a hat, as the event can be long and the weather warm.

What to Bring and Additional Tips

For summer events in New York City, it's essential to bring sunscreen, sunglasses, and water to stay hydrated in the heat. Comfortable shoes are a must, as many events involve standing or walking. A light jacket or sweater is also advisable for cooler evenings, especially if you're attending events that run late into the night. Lastly, arrive early to secure good spots, particularly for popular events, and consider packing snacks or a picnic for outdoor events where food options may be limited.

Fall Festivals

Fall in New York City is a magical time when the city is adorned with vibrant foliage, crisp air, and an array of festivals that celebrate the season. From cultural events to food festivals, autumn brings a diverse lineup of activities that showcase the city's rich traditions and creativity.

New York Film Festival

The New York Film Festival (NYFF) is one of the most prestigious film events in the world, attracting cinephiles and industry professionals. Held annually at Lincoln Centre, the festival features a selection of the best films from around the globe, including premieres, retrospectives, and experimental works.

Date

Late September to mid-October.

Dress Code

Smart casual: dress comfortably for sitting through screenings, but consider dressing up for premieres and special events.

Time

Screenings and events run throughout the day and evening.

Expect to see a diverse lineup of films, including feature films, documentaries, and short films. Tickets should be purchased in advance, as screenings often sell out. Bring a light jacket, as theatres can be cool, and consider arriving early to secure good seats.

Village Halloween Parade

The Village Halloween Parade is a legendary NYC event that takes place in Greenwich Village. This nighttime parade features thousands of participants in elaborate costumes, along with giant puppets, floats, and live music. It's a one-of-a-kind experience that draws huge crowds every year.

Date

October 31st (Halloween night).

Dress Code

Creative costumes are encouraged, whether you're in the parade or just watching.

Time

The parade starts at 7:00 PM and runs until around 10:30 PM.

Expect a vibrant, festive atmosphere with a mix of creativity and spookiness. Expect large crowds and street closures, so plan to arrive early and be prepared to stand for long periods. Bring a camera to capture the incredible costumes and floats.

NYC Wine & Food Festival

The NYC Wine & Food Festival is a four-day event that brings together some of the world's top chefs, winemakers, and food enthusiasts. Held in various locations across the city, the festival features tastings, dinners, cooking demonstrations, and more, with proceeds benefiting hunger-relief organisations.

Date

Mid-October.

Dress Code

Smart casual to business casual, depending on the event.

Time

Events take place throughout the day and evening, with some requiring separate tickets.

Expect a gourmet experience with opportunities to taste dishes from renowned chefs and sample a wide variety of wines. Bring a healthy appetite and be prepared to walk between venues. Tickets should be purchased in advance, as many events sell out quickly.

New York Comic Con

New York Comic Con is a major pop culture event that attracts fans of comics, movies, TV shows, and gaming. Held at the Javits Centre, the convention features panels, celebrity appearances, and an expansive exhibitor floor.

Date

October.

Dress Code

Cosplay is highly encouraged, with many attendees dressing up as their favourite characters.

Time

The convention runs from morning until evening, with some after-hours events.

Expect to see a lively, crowded environment filled with fellow fans. Expect long lines for popular panels and autograph sessions, so plan your schedule in advance. Bring comfortable shoes, as the Javits Centre is large, and you'll be doing a lot of walking.

Macy's Thanksgiving Day Parade

The Macy's Thanksgiving Day Parade is one of New York City's most iconic events, marking the start of the holiday season. The parade features giant character balloons, elaborate floats, marching bands, and performances by celebrities and Broadway stars. It's a beloved tradition that attracts millions of spectators both in person and on television.

Date

Thanksgiving Day, the fourth Thursday in November.

Dress Code

Bundle up in warm, comfortable clothing, as November weather in NYC can be chilly.

Time

The parade begins at 9:00 AM and lasts until about noon.

Expect large crowds and a festive, family-friendly atmosphere. Arrive early to secure a good viewing spot along the parade route, which runs from Central Park West to 34th Street. Bring along snacks, hot drinks, and a blanket or portable chair if you plan to arrive early and stake out a spot.

Thanksgiving Dinner

After the parade, many people enjoy a traditional Thanksgiving dinner at one of New York's many restaurants offering special holiday menus. These meals typically include turkey, stuffing, mashed potatoes, and other holiday favorites. Reservations are highly recommended, as restaurants fill up quickly for the holiday.

Expect a festive meal in a warm, welcoming atmosphere. Many restaurants offer prix fixe menus, which can range in price depending on the venue. Be sure to book your table well in advance to secure a spot at your preferred location.

What to Bring and Additional Tips

For fall events in New York City, it's wise to dress in layers, as temperatures can vary throughout the day. Comfortable shoes are essential, especially for events that involve standing or walking. A light jacket or sweater is recommended for cooler evenings. It's also a good idea to bring a reusable water bottle, as you'll want to stay hydrated while enjoying the city's festivities. Finally, arrive early to secure good spots, particularly for popular events like parades and festivals.

Winter Wonderland

Winter in New York City transforms the city into a magical wonderland, with a variety of festivals and events that celebrate the holiday season and the beauty of winter.

Rockefeller Centre Christmas Tree Lighting

The Rockefeller Centre Christmas Tree Lighting is one of the most iconic events of the holiday season. The massive tree, adorned with thousands of lights and a sparkling star, is officially lit during a televised ceremony that includes live performances.

Date

Late November or early December (date varies each year).

Dress Code

Bundle up in warm clothing; layers, hats, gloves, and scarves are essential.

Time

The ceremony typically starts in the evening around 7:00 PM.

Expect to see large crowds, festive music, and the excitement of the tree lighting. Arrive several hours early if you want a good view, or watch the event from a nearby restaurant. Be prepared for security checks, and bring along a thermos of hot cocoa to keep warm.

Holiday Markets

New York City's holiday markets are a must-visit during the winter season, offering unique gifts, handmade crafts, and seasonal treats. The most famous markets include the Union

Square Holiday Market, Bryant Park Winter Village, and the Columbus Circle Holiday Market.

Date

Typically from mid-November through December 24th.

Dress Code

Casual, but dress warmly as the markets are outdoors.

Time

Most markets are open from 10:00 AM to 8:00 PM.

You'll see festive stalls with a wide variety of products, like artisanal foods and handcrafted gifts. Bring cash or cards for purchases, and be sure to try the hot chocolate or mixed wine available at many vendors.

Ice Skating at Wollman Rink

Ice skating at Wollman Rink in Central Park is a quintessential New York winter activity. The rink offers stunning views of the city skyline and the surrounding park, making it a picturesque spot to glide on the ice.

Date

Typically open from late October through early April.

Dress Code

Wear warm, layered clothing, and consider waterproof gloves.

Time

The rink is open daily, with hours varying; typically 10:00 AM to 10:00 PM.

Expect to see a festive atmosphere with skaters of all ages and skill levels. Admission fees vary depending on the day of the week, and skate rentals are available. Bring your own skates to save on rental fees, and arrive early to avoid long lines.

New Year's Eve in Times Square

Celebrating New Year's Eve in Times Square is an unforgettable experience, with the famous ball drop marking the start of the new year. The event draws large crowds and includes musical performances, celebrity appearances, and plenty of confetti.

Date

December 31st.

Dress Code

Warm, comfortable clothing and plenty of layers; hand warmers and thermal gear are highly recommended.

Time

Arrive in the afternoon to secure a spot; the festivities start in the evening and continue until after midnight.

Expect large crowds, heightened security, and a lively, energetic atmosphere. Bring snacks, water, and anything else you might need, as once you're in the secured area, it's difficult to leave and return. Watching the ball drop is a bucket-list experience, so prepare for a long but memorable night.

What to Bring and Additional Tips

For winter events in New York City, it's essential to dress warmly and in layers, as temperatures can be freezing. Comfortable, waterproof boots are also recommended, especially if you'll be standing outside for long periods. Bringing a portable phone charger is a good idea, as your battery may drain quickly in cold weather. For popular events like the tree lighting and New Year's Eve, arrive early to secure a good spot, and be prepared for large crowds. Staying hydrated and keeping snacks on hand will make your experience more enjoyable, especially for longer events.

New York City's seasonal events and festivals showcase the spirit and cultural diversity that make the city so unique. Each season brings a fresh wave of celebrations, offering something special for everyone. These events are more than just dates on a calendar; they're experiences that bring the city's neighbourhoods, history, and traditions to life.

CHAPTER 11

Special Interest Tours

NYC offers an array of unique tours that cater to specific interests. These special interest tours are designed to go beyond the typical sightseeing experience, providing a closer look at the aspects of the city that might otherwise be overlooked.

Food Tours in New York City

New York City is a culinary paradise, and food tours offer an immersive way to explore its diverse neighbourhoods through their iconic and hidden culinary gems. These tours guide you through various eateries, markets, and speciality shops, providing both history and tastings that showcase the city's rich food culture. Whether you're a foodie looking to sample the best pizza or someone curious about international flavours, there's a food tour that caters to every palate.

Exploring Iconic Neighbourhoods

Many food tours focus on specific neighbourhoods known for their culinary diversity. For example, a tour of Greenwich Village might include stops at historic pizzerias, artisanal bakeries, and family-run Italian delis, while a tour of Chinatown could introduce you to dim sum, dumplings, and bubble tea. Each tour offers a taste of the area's history and cultural influences, making it both a culinary and educational experience.

Most food tours last between 2 and 3 hours, providing ample time to enjoy multiple tastings while walking between stops.

Tours are available across various neighbourhoods, including Greenwich Village, Chinatown, Little Italy, and more. The exact meeting point is usually provided upon booking.

Expect to visit 5-7 different locations, sampling everything from street food to gourmet treats. Along the way, your guide will share stories about the neighbourhood's history, architecture, and culture. Wear comfortable shoes, as you'll be walking between stops, and come hungry—these tours typically include enough food for a full meal.

Speciality Food Tours

For those with specific interests, speciality food tours focus on particular types of cuisine or culinary themes. For example, a pizza tour might take you to some of the city's most famous pizzerias, allowing you to taste and compare different styles, while a dessert tour could lead you through the best bakeries and sweet shops in town. These tours offer a deeper dive into a particular culinary tradition or theme, making them perfect for enthusiasts.

Time is typically 2-3 hours, though some extended tours may last longer.

Location varies by tour theme; pizza tours might focus on neighbourhoods like Little Italy or Brooklyn, while dessert tours could explore places like SoHo or the Upper West Side.

Expect in-depth tastings and discussions about the specific type of food being highlighted. Guides often share insights into the preparation techniques, history, and variations of the cuisine. Expect to walk and eat, with the opportunity to purchase additional items along the way if something particularly strikes your fancy.

What to Bring and Additional Tips

For food tours in NYC, dress comfortably, especially in terms of footwear, as most tours involve a fair amount of walking. Depending on the season, dressing in layers is a good idea to adjust to changing weather. It's also helpful to bring a bottle of water and some cash for gratuities or any additional purchases you might want to make.

Booking in advance is highly recommended, as food tours often sell out quickly, especially on weekends and during peak tourist seasons. These tours are an excellent way to experience the culinary diversity of New York City while learning about the history and culture of its neighbourhoods.

Art and Culture Tours

New York City is a global hub for art and culture, offering a rich tapestry of experiences that can be explored through specialised tours. These tours guide visitors through the city's renowned museums, galleries, and historic neighbourhoods, providing a deep dive into the artistic and cultural heritage of NYC. Whether you're interested in contemporary art, historical landmarks, or the vibrant street art scene, there's a tour to match your interests.

Museum and Gallery Tours

One of the best ways to explore New York's art scene is through guided museum and gallery tours. These tours typically cover major institutions like the Metropolitan Museum of Art (The Met), the Museum of Modern Art (MoMA), and the Guggenheim, as well as smaller galleries in neighbourhoods like Chelsea. Expert guides offer insights into the artworks, the history behind them, and the cultural context, making these tours both educational and engaging.

Tours generally last between 2 and 3 hours, depending on the institution or neighbourhood being explored.

Location is at major art districts like the Upper East Side for museums and Chelsea for galleries. Specific meeting points are provided upon booking.

Expect a curated experience with a knowledgeable guide who will take you through the highlights of the museums or galleries. Expect to walk through different sections with detailed explanations of key works. These tours are often interactive, with opportunities to ask questions and engage in discussions.

Street Art Tours

For those interested in contemporary and urban art, street art tours offer a chance to explore the vibrant murals and graffiti that decorate the city's neighborhoods. Areas like Bushwick in Brooklyn and the Lower East Side in Manhattan are famous for their street art scenes. These tours showcase works from both established and emerging artists, providing insights into the messages and techniques behind the art.

Time is typically 2 hours, though some can extend to 3 hours for more in-depth exploration.

Popular neighbourhoods for street art include Bushwick in Brooklyn and the Lower East Side in Manhattan.

Expect a walking tour led by a guide familiar with the street art community. You'll visit famous murals and hidden gems, learning about the artists and the cultural significance of the works. Bring your camera, as these tours offer plenty of Instagram-worthy spots.

Cultural and Historical Landmark Tours

New York City's cultural heritage is deeply intertwined with its history, and cultural tours often focus on historical landmarks, theatres, and neighbourhoods that have shaped the city's identity. These tours might take you through Harlem to explore its rich African-American history and jazz culture, or through Greenwich Village, known for its role in the LGBTQ+ rights movement and bohemian art scene.

Most tours last 2 to 3 hours, with some extending for half a day for more comprehensive explorations.

Location is in key cultural neighbourhoods like Harlem, Greenwich Village, and the Theatre District.

Expect a mix of walking and storytelling, with guides sharing the history, architecture, and cultural evolution of the neighborhoods. Expect to visit historic theatres, music venues, and significant landmarks. These tours often include stops at local cafes or eateries that are part of the cultural fabric of the area.

What to Bring and Additional Tips

When embarking on an art and culture tour in New York City, wear comfortable walking shoes and dress appropriately for the weather, as many tours involve significant walking. A camera or smartphone is essential for capturing the art and scenery, especially on street art tours. It's also a good idea to bring a notebook if you're keen on jotting down details or inspirations from the tour. Booking in advance is recommended, particularly for popular tours, to secure your spot.

These tours offer a unique way to experience New York City, providing a deeper understanding of the art, culture, and history that make the city so iconic. Whether you're an art enthusiast or simply curious about the city's cultural landscape, these tours are a fantastic way to enrich your visit.

Historical and Architectural Tours

New York City is rich in history and architectural marvels, making it a prime destination for those interested in exploring the stories behind its iconic buildings and landmarks. Historical and architectural tours offer a deep dive into the city's past, revealing how its architecture has evolved over the centuries and the historical events that have shaped it.

Exploring Iconic Landmarks

These tours often take you through neighbourhoods like Midtown Manhattan, the Financial District, and the Upper West Side, where you'll see some of the city's most famous buildings. Sites like the Empire State Building, the Chrysler Building, and the New York Public Library are commonly featured, along with lesser-known gems like the Woolworth Building or the Flatiron Building. The tours are usually led by knowledgeable guides who share fascinating insights into the design, construction, and historical significance of these structures.

Most tours last between 2 and 3 hours, providing ample time to explore several landmarks in depth.

Common starting points include Midtown Manhattan, the Financial District, and other historically significant areas. Specific meeting points are provided upon booking.

Expect to walk through the city's streets as your guide discusses the architectural styles, historical context, and cultural importance of the buildings you visit. These tours often include both exterior and, when possible, interior views of buildings. Wear comfortable shoes for walking and dress appropriately for the weather.

Historical Walking Tours

For those interested in the broader history of New York City, historical walking tours focus on specific neighbourhoods or events that have shaped the city. For example, a tour of the Lower East Side might delve into the history of immigration and tenement life, while a tour of Harlem could explore the Harlem Renaissance and the neighbourhood's cultural impact. These tours provide a narrative of the city's development, connecting architecture with the social and economic forces that have influenced it.

Time is typically 2 to 3 hours, with some extended tours offering half-day experiences.

Popular neighbourhoods for historical walking tours include the Lower East Side, Harlem, and Greenwich Village.

Expect a mix of storytelling and exploration, with guides providing in-depth historical context as you walk through the neighborhood. You'll visit key landmarks, hear stories of past residents, and gain a deeper understanding of how the neighbourhood has evolved. These tours are ideal for history buffs and those looking to connect with the city's past in a meaningful way.

Skyscraper Tours

New York City is famous for its skyline, and skyscraper tours offer an opportunity to explore the engineering feats and architectural styles that define it. These tours often focus on the tallest and most iconic buildings, such as the Empire State Building, the Chrysler Building, and the One World Trade Center. You'll learn about the challenges of building skyscrapers in a bustling city and how these structures have become symbols of New York's growth and ambition.

Most skyscraper tours are around 2 hours long, with some options extending to 3 hours for a more comprehensive experience.

Tours typically start in Midtown Manhattan or the Financial District, where many of the city's most famous skyscrapers are located.

Expect guided walks that highlight the design, construction, and cultural significance of New York's skyscrapers. Some tours include access to observation decks, offering stunning views of the city. Be prepared for some walking and potentially large crowds at popular sites.

What to Bring and Additional Tips

For historical and architectural tours in New York City, wear comfortable walking shoes and dress for the weather, as most tours involve significant time outdoors. A camera or smartphone is essential for capturing the impressive architecture, and a notebook may be useful if you want to jot down interesting facts or notes. Booking in advance is recommended, especially for specialised tours or those that include access to popular landmarks.

These tours offer a unique way to connect with New York City's past and present, providing a deeper appreciation of the buildings and stories that make the city so iconic. Whether you're marvelling at the grandeur of its skyscrapers or walking through historic neighbourhoods, these tours are an enriching experience for anyone interested in the history and architecture of New York City.

Ghost Tours and Spooky Sites

New York City is not just a bustling metropolis; it's also home to a number of ghostly legends and haunted sites. Ghost tours in NYC offer a spine-chilling way to explore the city's darker history, taking you through historic neighbourhoods, eerie buildings, and sites with a reputation for paranormal activity. These tours blend storytelling with historical facts, making them both entertaining and educational.

Ghost Tours of Greenwich Village

One of the most popular haunted tours is the Greenwich Village Ghost Tour. Greenwich Village is known for its rich history and charming streets, but it also has a reputation for being one of the most haunted areas in the city. This tour takes you to sites like the Merchant's House Museum, the oldest preserved building in Manhattan where ghostly apparitions have been reported.

Tours typically last about 2 hours and often start in the evening, around 7:00 or 8:00 PM.

The tour usually begins at Washington Square Park, a site with its own ghostly legends, and continues through the surrounding neighbourhood.

Expect a walking tour with stops at haunted buildings, former burial grounds, and locations with unsettling histories. Guides share stories of spectral sightings, eerie occurrences, and the historical context behind them. Dress warmly if taking the tour in the colder months, and wear comfortable shoes for walking.

Ghosts of New York Tour

The Ghosts of New York Tour offers a variety of routes focussing on different haunted areas, including Lower Manhattan and the East Village. These tours delve into the haunted history of sites like the New Amsterdam Theatre, where actors have reportedly seen ghostly figures, and the Morris-Jumel Mansion, known for its paranormal activity.

Most tours last 1.5 to 2 hours and are available in the evenings, with some special midnight tours for those seeking an extra thrill.

Location varies by tour, but common starting points include historic sites in Lower Manhattan and the East Village.

Expect a mix of ghost stories, historical facts, and visits to allegedly haunted sites. These tours are led by guides who specialise in the paranormal and New York history, offering insights into the legends that have persisted over the centuries. Be prepared for eerie tales and possibly a chill down your spine.

Haunted Broadway Walking Tour

For a unique twist, the Haunted Broadway Walking Tour takes you through the Theatre District, exploring the ghosts and legends of Broadway. From haunted theatres to stories of famous actors who never truly left the stage, this tour is perfect for those interested in both theatre and the paranormal.

This tour lasts about 2 hours, usually starting in the early evening.

It begins in Times Square and covers several theatres known for their ghostly reputations.

Expect an exploration of Broadway's haunted history, with stops at famous theatres like the Belasco Theatre, where the ghost of David Belasco is said to linger. The tour is a blend of theatre history and ghost stories, offering a behind-the-scenes look at the spookier side of Broadway.

What to Bring and Additional Tips

For ghost tours in New York City, it's important to dress appropriately for the weather, as these tours are mostly conducted outdoors and often in the evening. Comfortable walking shoes are a must, as you'll be on your feet for at least a couple of hours. A camera or smartphone is also recommended—you never know when you might capture something unexpected!

These tours are not just about the scares; they also offer a fascinating look at New York City's history, architecture, and culture. Whether you're a believer in the supernatural or just curious, these ghost tours provide a thrilling and educational experience that highlights a different side of the city.

Tours for Film and TV Buffs

New York City has been the backdrop for countless movies and TV shows, making it a paradise for film and television enthusiasts. Tours specifically designed for film and TV buffs take you to famous locations featured in your favourite shows and movies, offering a chance to see where iconic scenes were filmed while learning behind-the-scenes details.

On Location Tours

One of the most popular options is On Location Tours, which offers a variety of bus and walking tours dedicated to different movies and TV shows. From "Sex and the City" hotspots to "Gossip Girl" landmarks and Marvel's superhero locations, these tours provide an in-depth look at the places that have become part of pop culture.

Most tours last between 2.5 to 3.5 hours, depending on the specific tour.

Tours begin at various locations depending on the theme. For example, the "Sex and the City" tour starts near 5th Avenue, while the "Gossip Girl" tour kicks off at the Palace Hotel.

Expect a guided experience with stops at iconic locations from popular movies and TV shows. You'll visit spots where famous scenes were filmed, and your guide will share interesting trivia, behind-the-scenes stories, and the history of each location. Some tours also include opportunities to recreate scenes or take photos at the exact spots where your favourite characters stood.

Central Park Movie Sites Walking Tour

Central Park has served as the backdrop for countless films, making it a must-visit location for movie fans. The Central Park Movie Sites Walking Tour takes you through the park's most famous cinematic spots, from the boathouse in "When Harry Met Sally" to the bridge featured in "Home Alone 2."

This walking tour lasts about 2 hours.

The tour begins at the park entrance on 59th Street, near Columbus Circle.

Expect a leisurely walk through Central Park, stopping at various sites where movies were filmed. Your guide will point out locations and share stories about the movies and scenes shot there. It's a great way to see both the beauty of the park and its role in film history. Comfortable shoes are recommended, and be prepared for a moderate amount of walking.

Superhero Tour of New York

For fans of superhero films, the Superhero Tour of New York focusses on locations featured in movies from the Marvel and DC universes. You'll visit the Daily Bugle, the headquarters of The Avengers, and other key sites where your favourite superheroes have battled villains and saved the day.

This tour usually runs for about 2.5 hours.

It starts near Times Square and covers various locations around Midtown Manhattan.

You'll see a guided bus and walking tour that takes you to filming locations and sites important to the superhero genre. Expect to learn about the production of these films, the history of the characters, and the real-life locations that inspired comic book settings. The tour is family-friendly and ideal for comic book and movie fans alike.

What to Bring and Additional Tips

When joining a film or TV tour in New York City, be sure to wear comfortable shoes, as most tours involve a combination of walking and bus travel. Bringing a camera is a must, as you'll want to capture the iconic locations from your favourite shows and movies. It's also a good idea to bring a bottle of water and dress appropriately for the weather, as many tours operate rain or shine.

Booking in advance is highly recommended, especially during peak tourist seasons, as these tours are popular and often sell out. Whether you're a fan of classic films, modern TV shows, or superhero blockbusters, these tours offer a unique way to experience New York City through the lens of the entertainment industry. You'll not only see the city's famous landmarks but also gain a deeper appreciation for the role New York plays in the world of film and television.

These special interest tours in New York City offer a deeper and more personalised way to experience the city. They allow you to explore specific facets of New York that might otherwise go unnoticed, providing a richer and more meaningful connection to its history, culture, and character. These tours turn an ordinary visit into a unique adventure, leaving you with a greater appreciation of what makes New York City truly special.

CHAPTER 12

Shopping

New York City is a shoppersshoppers's paradise, offering an incredible variety of stores. The city's neighbourhoods each have their own unique shopping experiences.

High-End Shopping

New York City is synonymous with luxury, and its high-end shopping scene is second to none. For those seeking the finest in fashion, jewellery, and designer goods, the city offers a wealth of options that cater to even the most discerning tastes.

Fifth Avenue

Fifth Avenue is arguably the most famous shopping street in the world, lined with luxury boutiques and flagship stores. Stretching from 49th to 60th Streets, this iconic avenue is home to brands like Gucci, Louis Vuitton, and Tiffany & Co.

Location

Fifth Avenue, between 49th and 60th Streets, Manhattan.

How to Get There

Accessible via the B, D, F, andF, and M trains to 47-50th Streets-Rockefeller CentreCentre or the E, M trains to 5th Avenue-53rd Street.

Opening Hours

Most stores are open daily from 10:00 AM to 8:00 PM, though hours may vary.

Expect an upscale atmosphere with impeccably designed stores and world-class customer service. Shopping here is as much about the experience as it is about the products. Fifth Avenue is particularly famous for its elaborate window displays, especially during the holiday season.

Madison Avenue

Madison Avenue, running from 57th to 86th Streets on the Upper East Side, is another prime destination for luxury shopping. Known for its exclusive boutiques and quiet elegance, Madison Avenue offers a more intimate shopping experience compared to the hustle and bustle of Fifth Avenue.

Location

Madison Avenue, between 57th and 86th Streets, Manhattan.

How to Get There

Accessible via the 4, 5, 6 trains to 59th Street or the F, Q trains to Lexington Avenue-63rd Street.

Opening Hours

Typically open from 10:00 AM to 7:00 PM, with some stores closed on Sundays.

Expect a refined shopping experience where personalisedpersonalised service is the norm. Many of the stores here are smaller, more exclusive, and focused on luxury fashion, jewelleryjewellery, and accessories. Madison Avenue is ideal for those looking for a quieter, more sophisticated shopping trip.

The Shops at Columbus Circle

Located in the Time Warner CentreCentre at Columbus Circle, The Shops at Columbus Circle is a luxury shopping mall that offers a curated selection of high-end retailers, including Thomas Pink, Stuart Weitzman, and Tumi. The mall also boasts fine dining options and stunning views of Central Park.

Location

10 Columbus Circle, Manhattan.

How to Get There

Accessible via the A, B, C, D, andD, and 1 trains to 59th Street-Columbus Circle.

Opening Hours

Open Monday to Saturday from 10:00 AM to 9:00 PM, and Sunday from 11:00 AM to 7:00 PM.

Expect a modern shopping experience with a mix of luxury brands, gourmet food options, and convenient amenities like valet parking. The Shops at Columbus Circle is an excellent spot for those who want to combine shopping with dining or simply take a break with a view.

SoHo

SoHo, short for "South of Houston Street," is a chic neighbourhood known for its cobblestone streets and a mix of high-end boutiques and contemporary fashion brands. While SoHo has a more laid-back vibe compared to Fifth Avenue, it's still a hotspot for luxury shopping, with stores like Chanel, Prada, and Balenciaga calling the area home.

Location

SoHo, Manhattan (centred around Prince Street and West Broadway).

How to Get There

Accessible via the N, R, and W trains to Prince Street or the 6 train to Spring Street.

Opening Hours

Most stores are open daily from 10:00 AM to 8:00 PM.

Expect a trendier, more artistic shopping experience. SoHo is known for its unique mix of high-end fashion and cutting-edge design. The area is also dotted with art galleries and trendy cafes, making it a great place to spend an afternoon shopping and exploring.

What to Expect and Additional Tips

High-end shopping in New York City is not just about purchasing luxury items; it's about enjoying an experience that combines history, culture, and world-class service. Each area offers its own unique flavour of luxury.

Be prepared for a more relaxed pace in some of these neighbourhoods, where personalised service and attention to detail are key. Many stores offer private shopping appointments, custom fittings, and other bespoke services, so it's worth enquiring ahead of time if you're looking for something special.

New York City's high-end shopping scene is unparalleled, offering everything from timeless luxury to the latest in cutting-edge fashion.

Boutiques and Unique Shops

New York City is a treasure trove of boutiques and unique shops that offer a shopping experience far removed from the mainstream. These stores are often hidden gems, tucked away in vibrant neighbourhoods, and feature everything from indie fashion labels to one-of-a-kind home décor. Exploring these boutiques allows you to discover the creativity and diversity that define NYC's retail scene.

SoHo

SoHo is synonymous with boutique shopping, offering an eclectic mix of high-end designer stores and independent shops. The neighbourhood's cobblestone streets are lined with unique boutiques, art galleries, and specialty stores that cater to fashion-forward shoppers looking for something different.

The Lower East Side

The Lower East Side is a hub for edgy, offbeat boutiques that showcase the work of local designers and artisans. This neighbourhood is perfect for those who appreciate unique, handmade items and want to support small businesses. The area has a gritty charm and is home to some of the city's most creative shops.

Location

Lower East Side, Manhattan.

Address

Various, centred around Orchard Street and Ludlow Street.

How to Get There

Accessible via the F, M, J, and Z trains to Delancey Street-Essex Street or the B and D trains to Grand Street.

Opening Hours

Typically open from 11:00 AM to 7:00 PM, though hours may vary.

Expect to find indie fashion, vintage clothing, and unique accessories. The Lower East Side's boutiques are known for their individuality and focus on quality craftsmanship. The neighbourhood is also a great place to discover new designers and emerging brands.

East Village

The East Village is another neighbourhood brimming with character, offering a mix of vintage shops, quirky boutiques, and speciality stores. This area is perfect for those who love to browse through racks of vintage treasures or seek out rare and unusual items.

Location

East Village, Manhattan.

Address

Various, with popular streets including St. Mark's Place and 2nd Avenue.

How to Get There

Accessible via the L train to 1st Avenue or the 6 train to Astor Place.

Opening Hours

Most shops are open from 11:00 AM to 8:00 PM.

Expect to see vintage clothing stores, indie boutiques, and speciality shops offering unique finds. The East Village has a bohemian vibe, making it a great spot for discovering offbeat and creative fashion.

Brooklyn's Williamsburg

Williamsburg is known for its hipster culture and is home to a variety of independent boutiques that cater to trendsetters. From handcrafted jewellery to vintage furniture, the shops in Williamsburg offer a curated selection of unique items that reflect the neighbourhood's artistic spirit.

Location

Williamsburg, Brooklyn.

Address

Various, with key shops on Bedford Avenue and Grand Street.

How to Get There

Accessible via the L train to Bedford Avenue or the G train to Metropolitan Avenue.

Opening Hours

Typically open from 11:00 AM to 7:00 PM.

Expect to see vintage and contemporary boutiques, artisanal products, and handcrafted goods. Williamsburg's boutiques often focus on sustainability and ethical practices, making it a great place to find eco-friendly fashion and accessories.

What to Expect and Additional Tips

Boutiques and unique shops in New York City offer a shopping experience that's personal, intimate, and often inspiring. These stores are typically smaller, with carefully curated selections that reflect the owner's taste and passion. You'll find a wide range of price points, from affordable indie brands to high-end designer pieces.

When shopping in these neighbourhoods, it's a good idea to take your time and explore at a leisurely pace. Many shops have a laid-back atmosphere, allowing you to browse without pressure. Don't hesitate to chat with shop owners or staff—they're often passionate about their products and can provide great insights and recommendations.

These neighbourhoods are also known for their cafes, restaurants, and cultural spots, so plan to spend a full day exploring, shopping, and enjoying the local scene.

Flea Markets and Vintage Finds

New York City is a haven for those who love hunting for unique treasures and vintage finds. Flea markets and vintage shops across the city offer an eclectic mix of antiques, retro fashion, collectibles, and artisanal goods. Exploring these markets provides a nostalgic and often thrilling shopping experience where every item has a story.

Brooklyn Flea

Brooklyn Flea is one of the most famous flea markets in the city, known for its carefully curated vendors offering everything from vintage clothing and mid-century furniture to handmade jewellery and antiques. The market is an excellent spot to find one-of-a-kind items while enjoying the vibrant atmosphere.

Location

80 Pearl Street, Brooklyn (DUMBO location).

How to Get There

Accessible via the F train to York Street or the A, C trains to High Street.

Opening Hours

Saturdays and Sundays, from 10:00 AM to 5:00 PM.

You'll see a bustling market with over 100 vendors. Expect to spend a few hours browsing through the stalls, where you can find everything from retro furniture to quirky knick-knacks. The market also offers a variety of food vendors, making it a great place to grab a bite while shopping.

Chelsea Flea Market

Chelsea Flea Market is a must-visit for lovers of antiques and collectibles. Located in the heart of Manhattan, this market has been a staple for decades, attracting collectors and vintage enthusiasts alike. The market is smaller and more focused, making it easier to navigate and find high-quality items.

Location

29 West 25th Street, Manhattan.

How to Get There

Accessible via the F, M, N, and R trains to 23rd Street.

Opening Hours

Saturdays and Sundays, from 8:00 AM to 5:00 PM.

Expect to see a variety of vendors specialising in antiques, vintage clothing, art, and rare collectibles. Prices can vary, with some items being more high-end, but haggling is often part of the experience. The market has a friendly, community-orientated vibe, making it a pleasant place to shop.

Hester Street Fair

The Hester Street Fair is a unique outdoor market that combines vintage shopping with a street fair atmosphere. Located in the Lower East Side, the fair features a mix of vintage fashion, handmade crafts, artisanal foods, and local art. It's a great spot to discover emerging designers and enjoy a lively, creative environment.

Location

Hester Street at Essex Street, Manhattan.

How to Get There

Accessible via the F, M, J, and Z trains to Delancey Street-Essex Street.

Opening Hours

Saturdays from 11:00 AM to 6:00 PM (seasonal, typically April through October).

Expect to see vintage items, handmade goods, and food vendors. The fair often hosts special events, such as live music or themed markets, adding to the festive atmosphere. Expect to find unique fashion pieces, handcrafted jewellery, and delicious snacks.

Artists & Fleas

Artists & Fleas is a marketplace that showcases independent artists, designers, and vintage collectors. With locations in Williamsburg and Chelsea, this market is perfect for those looking to discover up-and-coming talent or find distinctive vintage pieces. It's a more curated experience compared to traditional flea markets, with a focus on high-quality, creative goods.

Location

88 10th Avenue (Chelsea Market), Manhattan; 70 North 7th Street, Brooklyn.

How to Get There

Chelsea: accessible via the A, C, and E trains to 14th Street

Williamsburg: accessible via the L train to Bedford Avenue.

Opening Hours

Chelsea: Daily from 11:00 AM to 7:00 PM

Williamsburg: Saturday and Sunday from 11:00 AM to 6:00 PM.

You'll see vintage fashion, handcrafted jewellery, art, and home décor. The market is indoors, making it a great option year-round. Vendors are passionate about their products, and you can often chat with them about their work. The Chelsea location is inside Chelsea Market, so you can easily combine shopping with a visit to the market's food vendors.

What to Expect and Additional Tips

Shopping at flea markets and vintage shops in New York City is about the thrill of discovery. Prices can vary widely, from affordable finds to more expensive antiques, but bargaining is common and often expected. It's a good idea to bring cash, as some vendors may not accept cards. Dress comfortably, as you'll likely spend a few hours walking and browsing.

These markets offer more than just shopping, they provide a chance to connect with the city's creative community, discover unique stories, and bring home a piece of New York's rich cultural tapestry.

Shopping Malls and Department Stores

New York City is home to some of the world's most iconic shopping malls and department stores, offering a wide range of options from luxury brands to everyday essentials. These venues are not just places to shop, they are destinations in themselves, often featuring dining, entertainment, and unique experiences that make them worth a visit.

Macy's Herald Square

Macy's Herald Square is one of the largest and most famous department stores in the world. Located in the heart of Manhattan, this historic store spans an entire city block and offers everything from high-end fashion to home goods.

Location

151 West 34th Street, Manhattan.

How to Get There

Accessible via the B, D, F, M, N, Q, R, W trains to 34th Street-Herald Square or the 1, 2, 3, A, C, and E trains to Penn Station.

Opening Hours

Monday to Saturday from 10:00 AM to 9:00 PM, and Sunday from 11:00 AM to 8:00 PM.

You'll see a massive selection of clothing, cosmetics, accessories, and home products. Macy's is known for its holiday window displays and annual Thanksgiving Day Parade. The store also offers personal shopping services and dining options, making it a convenient one-stop destination.

The Shops at Columbus Circle

The Shops at Columbus Circle is a luxury shopping centre located in the Time Warner Centre, featuring high-end retailers, gourmet dining, and stunning views of Central

Park. It's an upscale mall that caters to both locals and tourists seeking a premium shopping experience.

Westfield World Trade Centre

Westfield World Trade Centre is a shopping and dining complex located within the Oculus, a striking architectural structure in Lower Manhattan. The mall offers a blend of high-end and mid-range stores, making it a popular destination for both shopping and sightseeing.

Location

185 Greenwich Street, Manhattan.

How to Get There

Accessible via the 1, R, and W trains to Cortlandt Street or the E train to World Trade Centre.

Opening Hours

Monday to Saturday from 10:00 AM to 8:00 PM, and Sunday from 11:00 AM to 7:00 PM.

You'll see a mix of fashion, beauty, and technology stores, including Apple, Kate Spade, and John Varvatos. The Oculus itself is an architectural marvel, making it a popular spot for photos. The mall also offers a variety of dining options, from casual eateries to sit-down restaurants.

Bloomingdale's

Bloomingdale's, often referred to as "Bloomie's," is a high-end department store known for its fashionable selection of clothing, accessories, and home goods. The flagship store on 59th Street is a New York City institution, offering a quintessential shopping experience.

Location

1000 Third Avenue, Manhattan.

How to Get There

Accessible via the N, Q, and R trains to Lexington Avenue-59th Street.

Opening Hours

Monday to Saturday from 10:00 AM to 8:30 PM, and Sunday from 11:00 AM to 7:00 PM.

Expect a wide range of luxury brands, exceptional customer service, and personalised shopping experiences. Bloomingdale's is famous for its "Big Brown Bag" and often hosts in-store events and sales that draw shoppers from all over.

What to Expect and Additional Tips

Shopping malls and department stores in New York City offer a comprehensive shopping experience, combining a vast selection of products with dining and entertainment options. These venues are well connected by public transportation, making them easily accessible from anywhere in the city.

Expect to find a range of price points, from affordable to luxury, depending on the store and location. These shopping destinations often host seasonal sales, making it a good idea to check for promotions before visiting. Whether you're looking to splurge on designer goods or simply enjoy window shopping, New York City's malls and department stores provide a world-class retail experience.

Tips for Bargain Hunting in NYC

New York City might be known for luxury shopping, but it's also a fantastic place to score great deals if you know where to look. Bargain hunting in NYC is all about knowing the right places, times, and strategies to find quality items at a fraction of their usual price.

Thrift and Consignment Shops

Thrift stores like Beacon's Closet in Williamsburg and Housing Works in SoHo are great places to find gently used clothing, accessories, and home goods at a fraction of their original cost. These shops often carry a mix of vintage items and high-end designer pieces, making each visit an exciting hunt for unique finds. To get the best deals, try visiting during weekdays when stores are less crowded, giving you more time to browse and find hidden gems.

Sample Sales

Sample sales are a New York City staple for fashion enthusiasts. These sales typically feature designer items at significantly reduced prices, often up to 70% off. Brands clear out excess inventory, overstock, or last season's collections, offering shoppers the chance to pick up high-quality pieces without breaking the bank. Keep an eye on websites like Chicmi or NYC Sample Sales to stay informed about upcoming events. These sales are often held in pop-up locations in Midtown or SoHo, and it's best to arrive early for the best selection.

Street Markets

For a different kind of bargain hunting, explore NYC's street markets, such as the Canal Street markets in Chinatown. Here, you'll find an array of inexpensive goods, including souvenirs, accessories, and even knock-off designer items. Haggling is common in these markets, so don't be shy about negotiating for a better price. It's part of the experience and can lead to some great deals.

Outlet Shopping

If you're willing to venture outside of Manhattan, Woodbury Common Premium Outlets is a shopping mecca located about an hour from the city. With over 200 stores offering discounts on everything from luxury brands to everyday items, it's worth the trip for serious bargain hunters. The outlet mall also has additional sales during holidays, so plan your visit accordingly to maximise savings.

Timing and Strategy

Timing is crucial when bargain hunting in NYC. Weekday mornings are often the best time to shop, as stores and markets are less crowded, giving you a better chance to find great deals without the rush. Additionally, consider bringing cash, especially to smaller markets or thrift shops, as some places may offer better deals for cash payments and may not accept cards.

Be patient and enjoy the process. Bargain hunting in New York City is as much about the thrill of the find as it is about the savings. With so many options, from trendy thrift shops to bustling street markets, you're sure to discover something special at a price that won't hurt your wallet.

CHAPTER 13

Photography and Instagram-Worthy Spots

New York City is one of the most photogenic cities in the world, offering a wealth of iconic and hidden spots perfect for photography and Instagram-worthy moments. The city provides countless opportunities to capture stunning images that showcase its vibrant character.

Central Park

Central Park is a must-visit for any photographer, offering a wide range of picturesque scenes. The Bow Bridge, Bethesda Terrace, and the Central Park Mall are among the most popular spots. The park's natural beauty, combined with the backdrop of the Manhattan skyline, creates perfect compositions for both landscape and portrait photography.

Location

Manhattan, between 59th and 110th Streets.

Best Times

Early morning or late afternoon for softer light and fewer crowds.

Expect serene landscapes, seasonal flowers, and iconic landmarks. The changing seasons provide diverse photo opportunities, from blooming flowers in spring to vibrant foliage in the fall.

DUMBO and the Brooklyn Bridge

The DUMBO neighbourhood in Brooklyn offers one of the most famous photo spots in NYC—the view of the Manhattan Bridge framed by the red-brick buildings on Washington Street. The nearby Brooklyn Bridge Park provides additional stunning views of the Brooklyn Bridge and the Manhattan skyline, particularly during sunset.

Location

Washington Street and Water Street, Brooklyn.

Best Times

Early morning or sunset for the best light and fewer tourists.

Expect iconic views, waterfront parks, and cobblestone streets. The area is perfect for both wide-angle shots of the bridge and close-ups of the surrounding architecture.

Top of the Rock

For breathtaking aerial views of the city, the Top of the Rock observation deck at Rockefeller Centre is unbeatable. The 360-degree views include iconic sights like the Empire State Building, Central Park, and even the distant Statue of Liberty. This spot is particularly popular at sunset when the city's skyline is bathed in golden light.

Location

30 Rockefeller Plaza, Manhattan.

Hours

Daily from 9:00 AM to 11:00 PM (hours may vary).

Expect panoramic cityscapes and famous landmarks. For the best photos, visit during the golden hour or at night to capture the city lights.

The Vessel at Hudson Yards

The Vessel is a striking, honeycomb-like structure located in the Hudson Yards development. Its unique design and reflective surfaces make it a popular spot for creative photography. Climbing the vessel's interconnected staircases offers various angles and perspectives for dynamic shots.

Location

20 Hudson Yards, Manhattan.

Hours

10:00 AM to 9:00 PM (hours may vary).

Expect modern architecture and unique geometric patterns. Admission is free, but timed tickets are required, so plan ahead.

The High Line

The High Line is an elevated park built on a historic rail line, offering a blend of urban and natural elements. It provides excellent views of the Hudson River, city streets, and unique art installations. The park's design, with its mix of greenery and industrial architecture, makes it a great spot for both landscape and street photography.

Location

Runs from Gansevoort Street to 34th Street, Manhattan.

Best Times

Morning or late afternoon to avoid crowds.

Expect to see urban greenery, art installations, and views of the surrounding neighborhoods. The park's unique vantage points provide opportunities for creative compositions.

Tips for Capturing the Best Photos

Timing

Early morning and late afternoon (the golden hour) offer the best natural light for photography, with fewer harsh shadows and softer, warmer tones.

Weather

Overcast days can be great for even lighting, while clear days are ideal for capturing vibrant colours.

Equipment

Bring a wide-angle lens for capturing expansive views and a tripod for steady shots, especially during low-light conditions.

Patience

Popular spots can get crowded, so patience is key. Sometimes waiting a few extra minutes can allow you to capture that perfect shot.

New York City's iconic landmarks, stunning viewpoints, and hidden gems makes it a paradise for photographers. These locations offer endless possibilities for creating memorable images.

CHAPTER 14

Day Trips

New York City is surrounded by beautiful destinations that make for perfect day trips, offering a break from the urban hustle while providing a range of activities and scenic experiences. These day trips allow you to explore the region's rich diversity without venturing too far from the city.

The Hamptons

The Hamptons, located on Long Island's South Fork, is a popular destination known for its charming villages, stunning beaches, and upscale vibe. The area offers a mix of relaxation and outdoor activities, including beach outings, vineyard tours, and exploring local art galleries.

Location

The Hamptons, Long Island, New York.

How to Get There

Accessible via the Long Island Rail Road (LIRR) from Penn Station or by car (approximately 2-3 hours).

Expect to see beautiful beaches, quaint towns, and a laid-back atmosphere. Visit the local vineyards, browse through upscale shops, and enjoy fresh seafood at one of the many restaurants. The Hamptons is also home to numerous art galleries and cultural events, especially during the summer months.

While the Hamptons can be pricey, especially during peak season, day trips can be budget-friendly if you plan ahead, particularly if you bring your own picnic or opt for less expensive dining options.

Bear Mountain State Park

Bear Mountain State Park is a nature lover's paradise, offering hiking, picnicking, and boating opportunities just an hour north of Manhattan. The park is particularly popular in the fall, when the foliage transforms the landscape into a vibrant display of colours.

Location

Bear Mountain, New York.

How to Get There

Accessible by car (approximately 1 hour from NYC) or by Metro-North Railroad to Peekskill, followed by a taxi or shuttle.

You'll see scenic hiking trails, including a section of the Appalachian Trail, beautiful views of the Hudson River, and a historic inn. The park also features a zoo, a large outdoor pool, and picnic areas. In winter, there is ice skating available.

Entry to the park is free, though some activities like boating or the pool may have small fees. Bringing your own food and drinks can keep costs down.

Sleepy Hollow

Famous for Washington Irving's "The Legend of Sleepy Hollow," this historic town along the Hudson River is steeped in history and folklore. Sleepy Hollow is especially popular during Halloween, but it offers year-round attractions such as historic sites, scenic views, and charming village streets.

Location

Sleepy Hollow, Westchester County, New York.

How to Get There

Accessible via Metro-North Railroad from Grand Central Terminal (about a 40-minute ride).

Explore the Sleepy Hollow Cemetery, visit the Old Dutch Church, and take in the views from the riverside parks. During October, the town hosts various Halloween-themed events, including haunted attractions and lantern tours.

Entry to many sites is free or low-cost, though some special events may require tickets. The town also offers affordable dining options in its local cafes and restaurants.

Storm King Art Centre

Storm King Art Centre is an expansive outdoor sculpture park located in the Hudson Valley. It's home to over 100 large-scale sculptures set against a backdrop of rolling hills, meadows, and woodlands. The site is ideal for art lovers and those looking for a peaceful retreat.

Location

New Windsor, New York.

How to Get There

Accessible by car (about 1.5 hours from NYC) or by taking the Coach USA bus from Port Authority.

Expect to see a vast landscape dotted with impressive sculptures from artists like Alexander Calder and Richard Serra. The centre is great for leisurely walks, picnics, and enjoying the art in a natural setting. Bring comfortable walking shoes, as the grounds are extensive.

Admission fees apply, but the experience is well worth it. Pack a picnic to enjoy on the grounds to avoid extra spending on food.

Planning Your Day Trip

When planning a day trip from New York City, consider the travel time and transportation options, especially if you want to maximise your time at the destination. Many of these spots are best enjoyed with a relaxed schedule, allowing you to fully immerse yourself in the scenery and activities. Don't forget to check the weather forecast, especially if your plans include outdoor activities.

These day trips offer a refreshing escape from the city's fast pace, allowing you to experience the rich history, natural beauty, and cultural diversity of the surrounding region.

Other Practical Information

Health and Medical Services

New York City has an extensive network of healthcare facilities, including world-renowned hospitals such as New York Presbyterian, Mount Sinai, and NYU Langone. Pharmacies are widely available, often operating 24/7 in major neighborhoods. In case of a medical emergency, dial 911 for immediate assistance. Urgent care centres are a convenient option for non-life-threatening issues and are located throughout the city. It's advisable to have travel insurance that covers medical expenses, as healthcare in the U.S. can be costly.

Local Etiquette and Customs

New Yorkers are known for their directness and fast-paced lifestyle. While this might seem brusque, it's simply the city's way of efficiently navigating daily life. Politeness is still appreciated, say "please" and "thank you" and hold doors open when possible. Tipping is customary in New York, with 15-20% being the standard for services such as dining, taxi rides, and haircuts. When on escalators, stand on the right to let others pass on the left, and always allow people to exit the subway before boarding.

Language and Useful Phrases

English is the primary language spoken in New York City, though you'll hear a multitude of languages due to the city's diverse population. New Yorkers often use abbreviations, like "SoHo" for South of Houston Street or "NoMad" for North of Madison Square. While most people speak English, it's common to encounter Spanish, Chinese, and other languages in various neighbourhoods.

Religion

New York City is home to a wide array of religious communities, reflecting its multicultural population. There are places of worship for nearly every faith, including Christianity, Judaism, Islam, Buddhism, and Hinduism. Prominent religious sites include St. Patrick's Cathedral, the Islamic Cultural Centre of New York, and the Central Synagogue. Many places of worship offer services in multiple languages. Visitors are welcome at most religious sites, but it's important to dress modestly and be respectful of customs when entering.

Internet and Communication

Free Wi-Fi is widely available in New York City, particularly in public spaces such as parks, libraries, and even some subway stations. Many cafes, restaurants, and stores also offer free Wi-Fi to customers. For reliable internet access throughout the city, consider purchasing a local SIM card or using an international roaming plan. Communication apps like WhatsApp and Viber are commonly used for messaging. If you need to make a local call, public payphones still exist in some areas, though they are increasingly rare.

Accessibility

New York City has made significant strides in becoming more accessible, though challenges remain, particularly in older buildings and subway stations. Many attractions, hotels, and restaurants are wheelchair accessible, and the city's buses are equipped with ramps. The Access-A-Ride program provides transportation for individuals with disabilities who are unable to use public transit. Before visiting a specific location, it's wise to check their accessibility options. Central Park, museums, and major landmarks like the Empire State Building have accommodations for visitors with disabilities.

Currency Exchange and Banking

The currency used in New York City is the U.S. dollar (USD). Currency exchange services are available at airports, major hotels, and dedicated exchange offices throughout the city. ATMs are widely accessible and usually offer competitive exchange rates, though fees may apply. Major credit cards are accepted almost everywhere, but it's a good idea to carry some cash for small purchases, tips, or places that don't accept cards. Traveler's checks are less commonly used but can be cashed at most banks.

Emergency Contacts

In case of any emergency, dial 911 for immediate assistance with police, fire, or medical emergencies. Non-emergency situations can be handled by dialling 311, which provides information and services for city-related issues, including sanitation, public transportation, and noise complaints. Visitors should also be aware of their country's consulate or embassy contact information in case of a legal or travel-related emergency. Keep a list of important contacts, including your hotel's address and phone number, in case you get lost or need help.

General Tips

New York City is a walking city, so comfortable shoes are essential. The subway is the fastest way to get around, and a MetroCard will give you access to buses and trains. Be mindful of your belongings, as crowded areas can be targets for pickpockets. Drinking tap water is safe, and refill stations are available throughout the city, so carrying a reusable water bottle is a good idea. Be prepared for all kinds of weather, layering is key, as temperatures can vary throughout the day.

BONUS

Sample Itineraries

3-Day Itinerary for Visiting New York City

Day 1

Morning

Start your day early with a visit to Central Park. Enter through the 59th Street and 5th Avenue entrances and stroll through the park's southern end, exploring sites like Bethesda Terrace, Bow Bridge, and The Mall. Afterward, head to The Metropolitan Museum of Art (The Met) on the eastern edge of the park. Spend a couple of hours exploring its vast collections.

Late Morning/Early Afternoon

Exit the Met and take a short cab or bus ride down 5th Avenue. Stop by "St. Patrick's Cathedral" and then walk over to "Rockefeller Center." If the season is right, take a spin on the ice rink, or head straight to the Top of the Rock Observation Deck for stunning views of the city, including Central Park and the Empire State Building.

Lunch

Grab lunch at Rock Centre Café or explore the food court in the Rockefeller Centre concourse.

Afternoon

Post-lunch, walk over to the Museum of Modern Art (MoMA), just a few blocks away. Spend time exploring its impressive collection of modern and contemporary art. Afterward, take a leisurely walk towards Times Square to soak in the electric atmosphere and visit the many flagship stores.

Evening

Catch a Broadway show in the Theatre District. Before the show, consider dinner at Carmine's for a classic Italian meal or Junior's for their famous cheesecake. If you're not up for a full meal, grab a slice of pizza from Joe's Pizza nearby.

Day 2

Morning

Start your day with a visit to The Statue of Liberty and Ellis Island. Catch the ferry from Battery Park, which will take you first to Liberty Island and then to Ellis Island. Spend time exploring the museum and learning about the history of immigration to the United States.

Late Morning/Early Afternoon

Return to Manhattan and walk to the 9/11 Memorial & Museum. After paying your respects, head over to the nearby One World Observatory at the top of One World Trade Centre for panoramic views of the city.

Lunch

Have lunch at Eataly in the World Trade Centre complex or try Le District, a French-inspired market and food hall.

Afternoon

Cross over to Brooklyn via the Brooklyn Bridge. Once in Brooklyn, explore DUMBO (Down Under the Manhattan Bridge Overpass), known for its cobblestone streets and stunning views of the Manhattan skyline. Visit the Brooklyn Bridge Park for more photo opportunities and take a break with some ice cream at Brooklyn Ice Cream Factory.

Evening

Stay in Brooklyn for dinner at Juliana's Pizza or Grimaldi's for a classic New York pizza experience. If you have time, head to Brooklyn Heights Promenade for a nighttime view of the skyline before heading back to Manhattan.

Day 3

Morning

Begin your day with a visit to the American Museum of Natural History on the Upper West Side. Spend a few hours exploring the exhibits, including the iconic dinosaur halls and the Hayden Planetarium.

Late Morning/Early Afternoon

Head back across Central Park to the "Upper East Side" for some shopping along Madison Avenue. If art is more your style, visit the Guggenheim Museum for its stunning architecture and rotating art exhibitions.

Lunch

Lunch on the Upper East Side at Sarabeth's or The Mark Restaurant by Jean-Georges. If you prefer something more casual, try Shake Shack in Madison Square Park.

Afternoon

After lunch, head downtown to Greenwich Village for a more relaxed vibe. Walk around Washington Square Park and explore the boutiques and cafes in the West Village. If you're interested in history, consider a visit to The Tenement Museum on the Lower East Side, where you can learn about immigrant life in NYC during the 19th and early 20th centuries.

Evening

For your final evening, enjoy dinner in SoHo at Balthazar or Carbone for a classic New York dining experience. After dinner, walk through the lively streets of SoHo, known for its shopping and art galleries, or take a short ride to Chinatown for a late-night snack at Joe's Shanghai.

5-Day Itinerary for Visiting New York City

Day 1

Morning

Start your adventure at Central Park, entering through the 59th Street entrance. Wander through key spots like Bethesda Terrace, the Bow Bridge, and Strawberry Fields. Then, head to The Metropolitan Museum of Art for a couple of hours exploring its extensive collection.

Lunch

Stop for lunch at The Loeb Boathouse in Central Park or head to E.A.T. on Madison Avenue for a classic New York deli experience.

Afternoon

Walk down 5th Avenue to admire landmarks like St. Patrick's Cathedral and the Rockefeller Center. Visit the Top of the Rock Observation Deck for stunning city views. Continue to Times Square for some quintessential NYC photos and a visit to the many flagship stores.

Evening

Dine at Carmine's for hearty Italian fare or try Junior's for their famous cheesecake. Cap off the night by catching a Broadway show in the Theatre District.

Day 2

Morning

Begin at Battery Park and take the ferry to The Statue of Liberty and Ellis Island. Spend the morning exploring these iconic symbols of freedom.

Lunch

Return to Manhattan and enjoy lunch at Le District or Eataly in the Financial District.

Afternoon

Visit the 9/11 Memorial & Museum for a poignant reflection on the events of September 11th. Afterwards, head up to the One World Observatory for panoramic views of the city.

Evening

Walk across the Brooklyn Bridge to DUMBO. Explore the waterfront and have dinner at Juliana's Pizza or The River Café. Take in the skyline views from Brooklyn Heights Promenade before returning to Manhattan.

Day 3

Morning

Spend your morning at the American Museum of Natural History on the Upper West Side, where you can explore exhibits ranging from dinosaurs to space exploration.

Lunch

Grab a bite at Shake Shack in Madison Square Park or Sarabeth's on the Upper West Side.

Afternoon

Cross Central Park to the "Upper East Side" for a visit to the "Guggenheim Museum. After your museum visit, take a stroll down Madison Avenue for high-end shopping.

Evening

Head downtown to Greenwich Village. Enjoy dinner at Minetta Tavern or Carbone. Spend the evening exploring the village's vibrant nightlife or enjoying live jazz at Blue Note.

Day 4

Morning

Start your day in Williamsburg, Brooklyn. Explore the boutiques, vintage shops, and coffee spots along Bedford Avenue. Visit Smorgasburg if it's a weekend for a food market experience.

Lunch

Try one of the many trendy spots in Williamsburg, such as Maison Premiere for oysters or The Meatball Shop for a casual meal.

Afternoon

Head to Brooklyn Heights for a walk through the historic neighborhood. Visit the Brooklyn Historical Society or simply enjoy the views from the Brooklyn Heights Promenade. You could also visit Prospect Park and the nearby Brooklyn Museum for art and culture.

Evening

End your day in DUMBO or the Brooklyn Bridge Park area with dinner at Grimaldi's or The River Café. Enjoy the sunset and evening views of the Manhattan skyline from the park.

Day 5

Morning

Begin your final day with a trip to Harlem. Visit the historic Apollo Theatre and walk along 125th Street. Stop by the "Studio Museum in Harlem" or enjoy a peaceful moment in "Marcus Garvey Park.

Lunch

Have lunch at Sylvia's for classic soul food or try Red Rooster for a contemporary take on Harlem cuisine.

Afternoon

Head back downtown to explore The High Line. This elevated park offers unique views of the city and features public art and gardens. Continue to Chelsea Market for some shopping and snacks.

Evening

Wrap up your NYC visit with dinner at Buddakan in Chelsea or a rooftop dining experience at The Standard. If time permits, end the night with a walk along the Hudson River Park for a serene view of the city lights.

CONCLUSION

As your journey through New York City draws to a close, take a moment to reflect on the incredible experiences you've had. The city's energy, diversity, and iconic sights have likely created memories that will stay with you for years to come.

Before you depart, ensure all your travel arrangements are in order, and consider organising your photos to preserve the highlights of your trip. If you have time, write a few reviews to share your experiences and support the local businesses that made your stay special.

On your last day, enjoy a leisurely meal or a final walk through one of the city's many parks or along the waterfront. As you pack up, double-check that you have all your belongings and important documents, and take one last moment to appreciate the unique atmosphere of New York.

Your time in this vibrant city has likely expanded your horizons and left you with stories to tell. May the memories of New York City inspire your future travels and continue to resonate long after you've returned home. Safe travels, and may New York always hold a special place in your heart.

EVELYN BLAIR.

Printed in Great Britain
by Amazon

47473605R00185